St. Benedict's Guide to Improving Your Work Life

St. Benedict's Guide to Improving Your Work Life

WORKPLACE AS **WORTH**PLACE

Michael Rock

TWENTY THIRD PUBLICATIONS
www.23rdpublications.com

Twenty-Third Publications
1 Montauk Avenue, Suite 200, New London, CT 06320
(860) 437-3012 » (800) 321-0411 » www.23rdpublications.com

Cover images: Photo of office: iStock / Tjanze. Portrait of St. Benedict: detail, "Crucifixion with Saints" by Fra Angelico, Museum of San Marco, Florence, 1441-42 (public domain/The Yorck Project/Wikimedia Commons)

ISBN: 978-1-62785-121-3
Printed in Canada

DEDICATION

Over the centuries since the time of Benedict, education has been a primary apostolate of monastics. In fact, it has been said, with only moderate exaggeration, that the monks and nuns taught Europe how to read and write. Where Benedictines have been successful in education, it has been due, not only to their competence, but especially to their ability to provide an atmosphere of respect and concern for students as individuals. And this is communicated as much by example as by precept. Hearing about respect and sensitivity is never enough; it must also be experienced.

—Demetrius Dumm, O.S.B.[1]

CONTENTS

ACKNOWLEDGEMENTS

Many people have walked with me as I journeyed along over the years with my idea of the *worthplace* and its implications. I wish to give special thanks to Janice Rock, Reuven Bar-On, Michael Hughes, Daniel Hurtubise, Roger Keeler, Raymond Lahey, Augustus Meier, Judy Wyspianski, Denis Dancause, OMI, Kelly Nemeck, OMI, Jean-Jacques Serré, Michael Cox, Bernadette Gasslein, Richard Ladouceur, Claire Johnson, Ginette Pilon, Johanne Deschamps, Roch-André Leblanc, Bonita Slunder, Tracey Deagle, Josée Lajoie, David Johnson, Gilbert Labelle, Michel Manuel, Normand Brulé, + Noël Simard, Chris Dudley, Audrey Tremblay and Geoff Smith. A very special thanks to Joseph Sinasac, publisher, and Glenn Byer, associate publisher, Novalis Publishing, for believing in my project when they first discussed it with me. Thank you, finally, to Gillian Robinson, production editor, and to Anne Louise Mahoney, my editor, for their patience and skill in helping me.

PREFACE

… for some time now we too have reached
that turning point. …
This time, however, the barbarians are not waiting
beyond the frontiers,
they have already been governing us
for quite some time.
And it is our lack of consciousness of this
that constitutes part of our predicament.
We are not waiting for Godot, but for another –
and doubtless very different – St. Benedict.

—Alasdair MacIntyre, *After Virtue*[1]

While Alasdair MacIntyre was referring in the above quotation to the "barbarians" in the time of St. Benedict of Nursia (480–547), he also implied that "our predicament" today is just as barbaric and needs the infusion of insight from a *new kind* of St. Benedict. This book is an effort to address that need. My particular approach, as a retired professor of human relations, emotional intelligence and organizational behaviour for over 35 years, is to address the critical importance of personal awareness at work and in life. The challenge is to develop a *worthplace* – a workplace with values, personal dignity and ethical conduct.

The massive problem of workplace disengagement is at the heart of this challenge. Awareness and knowledge of the science of emotional intelligence are critical when it comes to addressing the challenge. The *Rule of Benedict*, written in the sixth century, offers an enlightening way to focus on this challenge and places it into a life-giving context.

This book gathers insights from my teaching, counselling experiences and personal life journey. I argue that we become that which we love, but we also become that which we hate. We *do* who we are. It is possible to build a new and "very different St. Benedict" today, but it will take confronting the barbarian – what Dr. Carl Jung called the Primitive Person – that lies within each of us so we can minimize its projection of blame that we do unto others for its existence.

The comic strip character Pogo put it correctly: "I have met the enemy and it is I." This book is about the grace and courage and humility we need to realize that the 'enemy' – MacIntyre's "barbarian" – first comes alive inside each one of us. The *Rule of Benedict* becomes a 1,500-year-old guide to being honest with ourselves and with others.

To facilitate this understanding, I have introduced concepts from my work in the theory and practice of emotional intelligence, specifically the scientific research of my friend and colleague Dr. Reuven Bar-On. With the help of the *Rule of Benedict* and insights from teaching and workshop experiences with Dr. Bar-On's Emotional Intelligence-*Inventory*™ (or EQ-i™), we are better able to address the challenges of employee disengagement: the role of emotions, which is at the heart of this problem, illustrates Benedict's own awareness of human relations.

My approach follows a conviction I have always held and taught: that *all change begins from the inside out*. To provide an overview, I begin, in the Introduction, by examining the global crisis of workplace disengagement today. I then follow up with key principles and ideas from the *Rule of Benedict*. There we find an interplay and discourse between the 'individual' and 'work.' When we go to our workplace each day, we do so as individuals. We *do* who we are. The first step is therefore to be conscious of who we are. To be engaged in our work is first of all a challenge to our inner selves – an emotional challenge, but also, as we will see, a spiritual one. Self-actualization is a major part of the journey to consciousness, but its innate tilt is to self-transcendence, the 'something more' that beckons us into a future worth going to.

A NOTE ABOUT THE TRANSLATIONS USED

I have used the following translations for any quotes from the *Rule of Benedict*: Timothy Fry, O.S.B. (Ed.), *RB 1980: The Rule of St. Benedict in Latin and English with Notes* (Collegeville, MN: The Liturgical Press, 1982); Terrence G. Kardong (Collegeville, MN: The Liturgical Press, 1981); Timothy Fry, O.S.B. (Ed.), *RB 1980: The Rule of St. Benedict in English* (Collegeville, MN: The Liturgical Press, 1982).

References to the *Rule of Benedict* are indicated within the text: for example, "P45" stands for Prologue, verse 45, and "RB 3.1" stands for *Rule of Benedict*, chapter 3, verse 1.

INTRODUCTION

THE *WORTH*PLACE CONTEXT

Your work is to discover your work
and then with all your heart to give yourself to it.

—Buddha

ack of employee engagement in the workplace is an enormous global challenge.[1] At its core, disengagement is an emotional challenge, but it is also a spiritual one. *Spiritual is understood here as the process of living life according to what one sees as ultimately important and meaningful.*[2]

TODAY'S DISENGAGEMENT CRISIS

Lily Tomlin is credited with saying that "the trouble with the rat race is that even if you win, you're still a rat." This prescient insight speaks to the chasing of the almighty dollar and of power and control. It's just not possible to feel authentically engaged in work or in life if money and power and control are your guides. Such an image of success is toxic to the workplace. Nigel Marsh cynically says that success is working long, hard hours at jobs we hate in order to earn money to buy things we don't need, in order to impress people we don't like.[3]

Employees experience disengagement when their workplaces are lifeless, dry as a desert, empty and barren. The prophet Ezekiel referred to such a condition as "dry bones" (37:1-14). T.S. Eliot said it was like "rat's feet over broken glass."[4] Take Ryan, a toxic senior manager who kept two fish tanks in his office. When someone 'messed up,' they had to take their favourite goldfish from one tank and put it into the other tank, which contained a piranha![5]

How bad is workplace disengagement? When Gallup uses the term "engaged," it means employees who work with passion, have a "profound connection" to their organization, and hence drive forward productivity and innovation. Gallup's 2013 research with 142 countries showed that only 13 percent of employees worldwide were truly engaged in their jobs. In Canada, 76 percent of the workforce is more or less *dis*engaged from their work; in the U.S., the figure is 75 percent. The worst is Japan, where 97 percent of workers are disengaged. Such extremes create havoc in the workplace and in people's personal lives. At best, employees get the work done somehow, but with minimal passion and commitment.

How can you recognize disengagement? Symptoms include *absenteeism / presenteeism*. Absenteeism is the physical absence of an employee; presenteeism means the person is present, but in body only, not in mind. Another symptom is *depression*. In 2003, the province of Ontario, Canada, spent $34 billion on workplace depression–related issues. A fourth symptom is *business ineffectiveness*. A 2013 Gallup State of the American Workplace survey found that actively disengaged employees were costing the U.S. $450 billion to $550 billion in lost productivity every year. Such ineffectiveness contributes both to a lack of creativity and to an absence of collegial thinking that can produce new ideas.

The 1927 silent movie *Metropolis*, about a Hades-like workplace, had this intertitle: "The link between the head and the hands is the heart." Employers have usually taken into account only intellectual factors in their hiring practices (e.g., IQ, academic scores) and are much slower to recognize the significance of emotions. Yet studies tell us it is precisely this oversight that is at the heart of the current disengagement gap. The Corporate Leadership Council report put it bluntly: "engagement … is driven dominantly by emotional factors."

Emotion is not a new reality. As early as 1872, Charles Darwin published his conclusion that *emotional awareness and emotional expression play a major role in survival and adaptation.*[6] In the 20th century, general intelligence came to be understood as "the capacity of the individual to act purposefully."[7] Dr. Reuven Bar-On realized that it is more accurate to refer to this wider construct as *emotional-social intelligence (ESI)*. Daniel Goleman, who has written widely on emotional intelligence, calls ESI "a new yardstick" and a "different way of being smart."[8] Most descriptions of EI or ESI include the ability to recognize and understand emotions, express feelings, understand how others feel and relate with them, manage and control emotions and strong feelings, manage change and resolve problems of a personal and interpersonal nature, generate positive affect and be self-motivated. EI has found a widespread application to many diverse situations – not only in personal life, but also in the workplace. Stunning research studies show that ESI fosters people, pride and profits.[9]

EI is also a bridge to the spiritual. St. Thomas Aquinas (1225–1274) wrote that "grace builds on nature." One needs a healthy nature to grow as a person, to experience self-transcendence, to move from being 'ego-centric' to being 'ex-centric' because we are built for greatness, for 'something more.'[10] Psychologist Abraham Maslow, at the end of his career, recognized that his widely accepted Hierarchy of Needs model – physiological, safety, love/belonging, esteem, and self-actualization – was incomplete.[11] He recognized a still higher motivation: self-transcendence. A 'something more,' in other words, was an intrinsic motivator in each of us. Perhaps it can be said that since EI deals with self-awareness and with what is meaningful, it offers a glimpse into the transcendence of the human person. In this way we can understand EI's place as a bridge to such spiritual phenomena as the inner journey, meaning and significance, wholeness and connectedness, and a sense of purposeful living. Of the many tools that can help us build this bridge to the spiritual, perhaps none can compare with the wisdom of the age-old *Rule of Benedict*.

REVALUING WORK: THE *RULE OF BENEDICT*

Our world today is not unlike the turbulent situation facing Benedict of Nursia (480–547 CE). His wisdom embraces work, life and human emotions; his spirituality provides insight into managing our own affairs. A missing ingredient when it comes to employee engagement is acknowledging the person doing the work. The prevailing tendency is to emphasize the work itself, thereby neglecting the one who does it. Pope John Paul II wrote that "the basis for determining the value of human work is not primarily the kind of work being done, but the fact that the one who is doing it is a person." In other words, *who workers are is work's subjective dimension; what they do is its objective aspect.*[12]

One of St. Benedict's enduring values is that he saw both sides: the value of the work, but above all the value of the worker. His contribution is all the more remarkable since his was an era of anarchy – in some ways, not unlike our own: the decline of Roman civilization, the onset of the Dark Ages, a time of conflict for the Church. In the midst of this chaotic situation, Benedict emerged as a true genius – a leader and a beacon of hope who was both deeply spiritual and profoundly human. His background was organizational; his early education was most likely intended to prepare him to become a government employee. However, he gave up his studies because he wanted to move away from the decadence he saw around him. After living for a while in strict solitude in a cave in the valley of Subiaco, Italy, he moved to Monte Cassino, where he built his first monastery. It was there that he wrote his *Rule*: a little gem of organizational genius and a healthy dose of common sense on how to approach and live life's realities.

Benedict fashioned his *Rule* "to establish a school for the Lord's service" (P45). But there is no reason we can't borrow his principles to provide guidance for the modern workplace. His monastery, being a school, was in essence an ongoing workshop with its living, progressive and experiential learning design. Work included prayer, sacred reading and physical work. This image of a school or workshop could be a paradigm for us today. The term "learning organization" is already popular in the business world. Expanding on this image can open up the shift to workplace as worthplace, because such a shift requires true relearning.

The Rule begins with one key word and three central principles. The key word is "*Obsculta*": to listen with the ear of your heart. Being a realist, Benedict had little time for listening only to make a response; that was arrogance. Listening, whose goal was learning and growing, required something very different: humility as reflected in being oneself, authentic, down to earth. Wholeness was found in the ordinariness of living with awareness and acceptance of human limitations as a form of truth, and thus a necessary springboard to growth.

A first principle was stability (*stabilitas*), best understood as rootedness, or, in the words of the modern saying, "Bloom where you are planted." Stability means attending to the present moment – as the Benedictine Joan Chittister would say, to live and work *here*, not someplace else. While such a posture could be used to defend the status quo, this was far from Benedict's thought. Stability asks us to stay *here* and not *there*, to focus on what needs doing *here*, not *there*, but also as the foundation for growth and change.

A second principle deals specifically with change. It is called conversion of life (*conversatio morum*). The idea is not at all static, but requires thoughtful openness and adjusting to the unpredictability of the "letting go/letting come" of daily living, as Goethe succinctly described the process.[13] For Benedict, that meant allowing one's behaviour to be shaped continuously by the monastic life, similar to a new employee's daily ongoing adaptation to the culture and social character of the work environment.

A third principle accompanying rootedness (*stabilitas*) and openness (*conversatio morum*) is obedience (*obœdientia*) – what we could call "deep listening." Many people today might react when they hear the word 'obedience' and think of subservience. This has little to do with the Benedictine concept. Benedict applied it to promptness in listening intently to the moment and to the signs of the times, to what we would call openness to feedback (e.g., 360°) personally and in the workplace. Obedience was a further implication of the *Rule's* opening word, "*Obsculta*," to create a sense of openness to getting at the truth about who you really are 'down *deep*.'

Central also to the *Rule* is its sense of balance, moderation and flexibility. Balance permeates the *Rule*. Obedience is offset by the right of appeal, and seniority by the recognition of the rights of the young.

Hospitality is tempered by provisions that guests should not upset monastic life. Stability has an equal emphasis on openness to change. The constant need to listen is balanced by the recognition of a time to speak (RB 7.56). The context is community, but also recognizing individuals as different. Flexibility is needed to account for different cultures, climates and conflicting interests.

Benedict was similarly farsighted in recognizing the importance of interpersonal relationships. Genuine spirituality embraced the inner dimension, but extended to life's relationships. In community, a monk's mettle was tested, for he came face to face with himself, his relationships, and his own strengths and weaknesses. What today psychologists call 'projection', or seeing in the other a part of what is also in oneself – whether positive or negative – surfaces very quickly in community life. Benedict's approach was to respect humanity and personal dignity, setting down "nothing harsh, or oppressive" (P46). Patience requires not only caring for oneself, but also caring for the good of others, often their weaknesses, whether in body (sickness) or in behaviour (RB 72.5). Ultimately, however, if implicitly, Benedict's spirituality of community rested on a still higher principle – the notion of respect for the divine presence in each individual and the connectedness to others, to creation and to God that this entailed.

Benedict was adamant that a community have humane leadership. The abbot was not only the leader of the community, but an exemplar for it (RB 2.12). He must learn to manage his own emotions, such as restlessness, feeling troubled, going to extremes, being headstrong, jealous or overtly suspicious. As leader, the abbot had to respect the diversity of individuals, accommodating and adapting himself to each person's character and intelligence, bringing out the best in each individual – a model not unlike that of the servant leader that is often advocated for today's workplace. A leader could never be a one-size-fits-all problem solver. Benedict constantly promoted the spirit of discernment, the ability to recognize the essential in a person or a situation with its implicit sense of contextuality: what is a good decision in one context may not be so in another. Benedict knew that order brought peace, but he recognized that change was a part of life. It was vital to recognize which of these should have priority. Very critically, Benedict recognized that leadership comes not from omniscience but from a human being who, like everyone else, is wounded.

Consequently, the *Rule of Benedict* is distinguished by being both sensitively personal and shrewdly organizational in its scope. It focuses on how monks should live, their duties and responsibilities, the hierarchy among them and the orderly administration of the monastery.

Benedict was straightforward in crafting leadership and self-management principles for the monks to follow, under the overall leadership of the abbot. But even here, Benedict obviously understands and recognizes the human and emotional dimension of what he is proposing. His flexibility is founded on the principle of subsidiarity: that in an organization, a problem ought to be tackled by the level closest to it, usually the lowest level possible. Much of the responsibility of senior monks would involve facilitation and the channelling of resources, but always with a certain hands-off approach. That allowed every individual to participate in the management of the community, and none is reduced to the status of just being a resource.

Benedict's *Rule* is pervaded by practicality. While an element of asceticism is always present, Benedict's spirituality focuses not on some mystical experience, but on the lived realities of each day. He divided the day into various portions, which is another of his legacies: sufficient hours for sleep; time for prayer; time for reading the Scriptures and spiritual writings; five hours of manual work – whether domestic, craft work, or work in the garden or fields. He offers a balance of prayer, work, and study and rest. The monks were to have clothes suited to the climate; those who were sick or elderly were to have sufficient food and drink. His is a spirituality that, although communitarian, is also eminently personal. There is a sense that life should bring personal well-being. He encourages his monks not to run away because of difficulties, for in following his counsels they will experience an "unspeakable sweetness of love" (P49).

Those familiar with the Benedictine tradition know that its emphasis on hospitality is legendary. Hospitality and worth are integrally linked realities. Every guest, especially one who was poor, was to be received as Christ (RB 53.15). Benedict writes that when guests show up, monks "should hurry" (*occurratur*) to greet them. Benedictine hospitality clearly reflects personal recognition and human dignity and sees worthiness in the stranger, even when the rest of the culture does not. For the great spiritual writer Henri Nouwen (1932–1996), hospitality meant "primarily the creation of a free space where the stranger can enter and become a friend instead of an enemy."[14] This "free space" is essential to learning and to respecting the learner.

The *Rule* can also be more directly related to today's workplace. It has established both personal and organizational principles that have endured for centuries. Chapter 48 is simply called "Daily Manual Labour" and begins with the now famous words "Idleness is the enemy of the soul." Idleness may mean 'loafing,' but it has more to do with the notion of availability and with rejecting an "I-don't-care" attitude – a very real sense of disengagement. In Benedict's day, work was more than a remedy for idleness. It was an important part of life and one's calling, as well as being utilitarian and purposeful. Benedict's approach to work had several key characteristics:

Work has its own value. The instrumentalist attitude of many contemporaries – "I only work for such-and-such an objective" – has no part in Benedict's thought. Benedict believed in excellence, doing whatever the work was and doing it well. Work has value in and of itself; it gives meaning to the worker. The effort to do a good job, respecting people, places and things – an ethic of diligence, care and respect – is a virtue in itself. Benedict saw work as a vocation, a calling, a part of life. He makes this abundantly clear: "they are then truly monks when they live by the labor of their hands, as did our fathers and the apostles" (RB 48.8).

Work is service. Inherent in work is a deep sense of social responsibility. Monks work to be economically independent and not a burden to others in society. Work has a God- and other-centred purpose; it not only benefits the self but also focuses on acts of charity for the neighbour, welcoming and attending to guests and strangers, not turning them away, and giving alms to those in need (RB 4.25-26). It includes the necessary labour of taking care of the sick and providing for monks who can no longer work. For Joan Chittister, "In the monastic tradition, work is for giving, not just for gaining [because] other people have a claim on what we do. Work is not a private enterprise. Work is not to enable me to get ahead; the purpose of work is to enable me to get more human and to make my world more just."[15] Such a vision expresses the humanism, the respect for the individual and the social responsibility that are essential to Benedict. Perhaps nothing today could be so countercultural. To be lazy and irresponsible are signs of "injustice and thievery," taking "from the people of the earth."[16] In a Benedictine vision, ecology acknowledges that the earth and its peoples are not here to care for us; we are here to care for them. Work develops us and makes time worthwhile.

Work is community. Benedict teaches us that work is our gift to the world, our social fruitfulness, done in community. Herbert Applebaum, an historian of work, has observed: "The Benedictine system demonstrated how efficiently daily work could be done when it was collectively planned and ordered, when there was cooperation rather than coercion, and when the whole [person] was employed."[17] Work allows us to focus on something other than ourselves, and in that way draws us away from self-centredness.

Work builds the person. Norvene Vest, a Benedictine oblate and spiritual writer, writes that work is the friend of the soul.[18] She says that the Benedictines remind us with their spirituality that we are missing something: the *Rule* can teach us that within the work itself is something life-giving and necessary to living life well. Work builds a sense of personal worth. Dutch professor Wil Derkse, who writes about Benedictine spirituality, goes so far as to say that the "quality of my work and the condition of my soul are intimately connected. My work expresses how my soul is faring."[19]

Work is prayer. While this phrase is not found in the *Rule*, the Benedictine motto is "Prayer and Work," with the two activities always conjoined. Benedict wants his monks, in their work, to keep God's presence – hence, a vision of self-transcendence – always before them. There is always a higher value at work, literally and spiritually.

Work is prophetic. For Benedict, work was the great equalizer, with physical labour acting as an equal obligation for each individual. In its simplicity and its classlessness, Benedict's notion of work offers an ongoing challenge to any society that adores the gods of consumerism, egoism, individualism, efficiency and profit for profit's sake.

It is doubtful that any other approach to work integrates work into the whole of human life as does Benedict's *Rule*, which treats work in such a holistic manner. And within Benedict's context, of course, work being integral to life makes work integral to the spiritual journey. Of its nature, to work well is to be spiritually healthy. This elevates work and endows it with a character of ultimacy, making work purposeful because it is directed toward an ultimate end. This transcendent character reinforces its connectedness. Work is a community effort, but much more than this, since in the end, work involves a responsibility not only to one's immediate neighbour, but to the entire universe – literally, to all that exists. While other approaches to the workplace certainly contain some of these elements, they usually fall far short of Benedict's, which sees work in terms of such genuine majesty.

1

WORK AS A CALLING: MATURITY AND STABILITY

[People's unhappiness] arises from one single fact,
that they cannot stay quietly in their own chamber.

—Blaise Pascal, *Thoughts in Solitude*

Oh, how restless we are! Benedict noticed this even in his own day: a person's proclivity to keep moving around. He mentions how "detestable" were the monks called "sarabaites," because without a clear rule they were aimless, "soft as lead" (RB 1.6). We would say today that they 'bent with the wind.' In the 1960s there was a sign that read: "Just don't do something; stand there!" This quasi-Buddhist slogan meant to convey the idea that constant movement did not bring inner peace. Stability did.

Benedict had tremendous insights into human nature. He knew that restlessness decentred a human being. In Jesus' parable of the sower, the seeds that didn't take root didn't have a chance to grow and bear fruit. Today's business lexicon is proud of an employee's ability to "multitask," despite studies showing that this approach negatively affects memory and energy. Benedict would not have known the word, but he was concerned about his monks constantly being on the go, whether mentally, physically, psychologically or spiritually. He had little patience for such dehumanizing effects on life and work. "No focus, no growth," he might have written. At the heart of his *Rule's* emphasis on stability is his emotional and spiritual insight of rooted-ness as a basic human need.

The workplace today seems to put emphasis on 'employee flex-ibility' – often understood by employees as fearing for their jobs unless they agree to be moved or downsized. Still, one Benedictine commentator highlights the shadow side of flexibility – insecurity and the lack of roots. He points out that psychologically, this creates depression, which he describes as "the soul's protest against this flex-ibility."[1] For some people, time – a key factor in stability – has lost meaning. Time is monitored instead by emails and cell phones, by the ticker tape in the lobby of one company where employees knew that the stock market numbers had to be higher at the end of each day. People no longer come to work from an interior zone of rootedness, of being and living who they truly are.

Benedict clearly saw work, like life itself, as a calling. Perhaps to put it even better, he saw life as a calling to which work was integral. At Carl Jung's hermitage in Böllingen, where he took quiet time for himself, a sign read: "*Vocatus atque non vocatus, Deus aderit.*" That is, "Called or not called, God is present." Benedict would heartily agree, but he also recognized the other side of the same coin: "Whether you know it or not, you have been called." He would maintain that every human being has a calling, whether or not it is recognized. Stability gives us both the grounding and the context for living out our call.

When life and work are experienced as calling, something different happens. Being truly connected with ordinariness, the "here and now" or the depths of daily living, has not only an external dimension but an interior one. The inner reassurance that comes from rootedness creates not only this zone of interiority but also the external calm needed to be engaged. Interiority allows a person to put that wonderful sense of gracefulness, both emotionally and spiritually, into all they do. While we would never claim that it provides for total calmness, it does provide a perspective to embrace more easily the ups and downs of ordinary living and working. In the workplace, the intense distractions that affect today's employees destabilize them, thereby disordering them. If there is anything Benedict wanted, it was order: a time and a place for everything. Such order allowed for human growth and the maturation process. Short of such order, people would get caught up in the busyness of daily life and its demands rather than first developing an interior listening. The Canadian Catholic philosopher Jean Vanier calls this busyness "feverish activity."[2]

Stability is wedded to maturity. It is by having a fixed point of growth (stability) that one is able to mature, since our inner self must keep informing our conscious self in order to stay balanced. A commitment to stability helps us acknowledge on an ongoing basis that all personal change happens inside out (what Benedict called *conversatio morum*). Immaturity can thus be seen as the lack of any inner ordering principle – a person at the mercy of the wind! To forget or disavow the intuition and thus the embrace of an inner life is to begin a hollowing-out process rather than a process of maturation. Irshad Manji, a Canadian journalist and Muslim, quotes a Koran warning that says, "God changes not what is in a people until they change what is in themselves."[3] Understanding work as a spiritual call can come only from such interiority. Our vision must embrace the notion of wholeness. Stability commits us to that connectedness that ties and links us to self, to others and to the wider world around us. For Benedict, engagement and interiority were seen as in a mutual embrace.

Without this interiority, this inner connectedness, work cannot be experienced as *calling*. The process involved is a maturing one, for sure, and is "ex-centric," a process going beyond a person's ego concerns to the 'other.' If this does not happen, a person stays locked into their own set of preoccupations without concern for what is beyond their immediate circumstances. Individualism then becomes the dominant factor, a world-view of me, myself and I. But true growth and maturity is not all about me. It's about Benedict's notion of working "from an attitude of humility,"[4] his idea of being realistic, down to earth, what today we would call being real, not phony or plastic, or in T.S. Eliot's word, "hollow."[5] Pierre Teilhard de Chardin, a French philosopher and Jesuit priest (1881–1955), says it all so well when he writes: "There is an almost sensual longing for communion with others who have a larger vision. The immense fulfillment of the friendship between those engaged in furthering the evolution of consciousness has a quality impossible to describe."[6] This larger consciousness is what the wisdom of Benedict's *Rule* proposes to us.

Work today is a developmental progression from what Benedict saw as a visible commitment and demonstration of one's spirituality. Work stemmed from deep-rooted (think *stabilitas*) links to the community, visibly manifesting a dedication to God, honouring God-given talents, serving God and the neighbour to whom they were tied by bonds of love. This awareness of work's original integrity and purpose is very important to understanding work today as a spiritual calling. The word 'integrity' is very deliberately chosen, because in its etymological roots is the mathematical notion of integer, or 'one,' suggesting the notions of oneness and wholeness. Thus, to keep work's integrity for today's employees is to reaffirm this vision of unity of personhood rooted (*stabilitas*) in their very need to be and become all they were called to be.

Distractions, as we have seen, are the idols that seduce us away from a trusted path in life and affect employees and workplaces globally. Former Benedictine Abbot Christopher Jamison of Worth Abbey in England says that distractions of the mind are also noises inside one's heart.[7] Such noises can be constant and deadening to a person. I view these noises and idols as the four Ps: *Persona* (seducing us to believe that image is everything); *Profit* (seducing us to believe that quantity outperforms everything); *Power* (seducing us to believe that control is ultimate); and *Prestige* (seducing us to believe that fame equals significance).[8] Especially in combination, but even individually, these idols create the context, or social character, so prevalent in today's *disconnect*: that is, the disengagement of *work* from *worth*.

While the *Rule* contains numerous clues that can help us view work as a calling, the three main anchors that Benedict establishes as grounds for the monastic experience (which I mentioned in the Introduction) are fundamental: *stabilitas* (rootedness), *conversatio morum* (ongoing engagement and openness to change), and *obœdientia* (obedience, understood as the deep and inner art of listening). These three values, of course, are vital not only to the workplace, but also to families and society at large. Benedict's is a spirituality for life that has stood the test of time because it is founded on the essence of being human. Everything doesn't have to be done at once, but there must be an openness to such energy, to such a spirit, to the possibility of developing hearts of "flesh" rather than of "stone" (Jer. 32:39).

In the same context, it is essential to recognize that Benedict never considered his *Rule* as a set of regulations that one simply adheres to. If that happens, it then loses its "salt" (Matt. 5:13), its flavour, becoming legal rather than holistic. Life today, as Sister Joan Chittister remarks, "is no longer a matter of either accepting destiny or simply following patterns set for us by generations long past. It is now the basis of the spiritual quest, the wholeness of the soul. Now we take ourselves seriously, as well."[9] In other words, we must have the courage and honesty to "unmask the self to the self."[10] Peter Sellers, who played many comic movie parts, once said: "There used to be a me behind the mask, but I had it surgically removed."[11] But he was wrong. There is an enduring 'me' inside each of us! Benedict wanted this 'me' to unfold organically in community for working and for living and wanted people to spend their lifetime making that happen.

A good metaphor to get an image of this inner journey is to think of the time you may have started lessons to play a musical instrument. I remember my grandson at the age of two simply hitting one note continuously. After a while, one's hearing was, to put it mildly, challenged. But as he got older, his parents gave him piano lessons, and music by Chopin started to emerge. What delight! Analogously, in developing a sensitivity and a practice – because it does take practice – to paying attention to one's interiority, there comes the incredible dimension of joy about one's inner world. With time and practice, attentiveness in these ordinary details of daily living becomes a habit.[12] A remarkable quote that is so pertinent to the need for an inner life comes from Warren Buffet, the investment guru and philanthropist: "I insist on a lot of time being spent, almost every day, to just sit and think. That is very uncommon in American business. I read and think. So I do more reading and thinking, and make less impulse decisions than most people in business. I do it because I like this kind of life."[13] Mahatma Gandhi saw the end results of interiority in even broader terms:

Your beliefs become your thoughts,
Your thoughts become your words,
Your words become your actions,
Your actions become your habits,
Your habits become your values,
Your values become your destiny.[14]

Developing such interiority is a great challenge. Jung's maxim still bears repeating: "Called or not, God will be there." Even if one is not consciously open to the spiritual, the task for self-development – a spiritual task – will still be there. For those who choose to open themselves to work's spiritual calling, no more poignant intuition could be spoken than that by Paul Valéry, the French poet, essayist and philosopher: "A great silence listens and I hear hope." Benedict's *Rule* opens up the grandeur and joy of a maturational process. Because we have chosen commitment to the process, to the call, work becomes transformed. So does life itself.

In short, practising *stabilitas* or being rooted in inner values will foster alertness to the everyday around us; we will begin to notice what's happening. For Benedict, listening – paying attention and noticing – are fundamental conditions that provide the necessary context for the three values described above to flourish. Little by little, what we notice and value becomes what is of worth to us. What is true generally is true of employees in their workplaces.

Benedict opens his chapter on work with this famous line: "Idleness is the enemy of the soul" (RB 48.1). With his sense of calling, work – even what might be regarded as the lowliest kind of work – and a spiritual life were tied together. The Benedictine saying "*Ora et Labora*," or "Prayer and Work," included three dimensions for the monastic life: (1) prayer, (2) *lectio divina* (reflective reading), and (3) physical work. Transposing the same conditions to a more general setting translates into a similar model: (1) focusing one's attention first on what is most fundamental, (2) pondering the factors going on in life, and (3) doing actual work in a clear and focused manner. Work, given these three dimensions, contains its own "ascesis," or ascetical dimension. It becomes part of a "life in the spirit."

The way forward to experiencing work as a spiritual call starts with true listening. Listening is this deepening experience to our inner selves. When we do begin to listen, we become conscious of those deeper intuitions that life is bringing to us. When it comes to work, we begin to see the outlines and then the more meaningful contents of what life opens us to within the workplace. We learn how important faithfulness is to our intuitions. We start being rooted, and we learn, little by little (*conversatio morum*), to both shape our commitments and allow them to shape us and our vision. Little by little, we also become whole, because we become more of who we are. That's the purpose of the human journey in the first place.

In more concrete terms, as both Blaise Pascal and Warren Buffett remind us, that journey begins in the quiet of our own rooms.

2

WORKING TOGETHER: WORK AND COMMUNITY

No man is an island, entire of itself;
every man is a piece of the continent, a part of the main. ...

—John Donne, "No Man Is an Island"

From the early days of the Internet, it was amazing to see the many home pages people created. Email, instant messaging and blogging, then Facebook, Twitter and many other similar tools, quickly followed. It seemed as if connectedness and belonging had become the world's great driving forces. The phenomenon touched young and old alike, in their personal, social and professional life. The difficulty seems to be that the attention to a virtual community functions often to the detriment of the real-life community closer at hand.

The heart and soul of Benedict's world was community, but very definitely a living one. Benedict knew how important good human relations were even for personal well-being. He came to realize that 'sandpaper living,' where people rub up against one another on a constant basis, was a healthy component of life, a context ideal for personal growth, both emotional and spiritual.

But what makes community? Some have an idealistic picture of community; however, Jean Vanier puts such idealism into perspective in urging us to move beyond the ideal:

The ideal doesn't exist. The personal equilibrium and the harmony people dream of come only after years and years of struggle, and then only as flashes of grace and peace. Peace is the fruit of love and service to others. I'd like to tell the people in communities, "Stop looking for peace. Give yourselves where you are. Stop looking at yourselves, look instead at your brothers and sisters in need. Ask how you can better love your brothers and sisters. Then you will find peace."[1]

Benedict also offers an incredibly simple but challenging description: in community, one is constantly anticipating what is better for someone else. This idea was such a priority for him that he even wrote of community as a competitive experience: that is, its members should try to outdo one another in respecting others (RB 72.4). Community was clearly not something superficial. For Benedict, community demanded four key and challenging coordinates: respect, patience, openness and action.

Respect: Benedict's demand for justice within the community called for constant fairness. To avoid one-upmanship, Benedict decided that rank was determined by a monk's date of entry into the community, and not by age or earlier position. Moreover, the abbot was not to play favourites (RB 2.16). Candidates for higher positions were to be assessed on "the merit of their lives and the wisdom of their teaching" (RB 21.4).

Fairness required a true respect for the other, which allowed the other to be who they were. It showed a reverence for their person. Fairness is the opposite of discrimination – not because of any legal requirement, but because it recognizes personal dignity. It also involves not projecting unconscious contents onto other individuals and not wanting to change them into what we think they should be, even in the name of 'helping,' which often meant 'rescuing' instead, eventually leaving the other person helpless and dependent. We 'help' a person who truly needs assistance; we 'rescue' a person because it suits us by making us feel needed or important. In fact, this would be the shadow side of respect, a pretense that actually dishonours the other psychologically and spiritually.

In today's workplace, lack of respect often has to do with idle conversation, a factor Benedict specifically recognized. The expression that "sticks and stones may break my bones but names will never hurt me" is simply untrue. Names *do* matter; discourse can be either hurtful or healing. To say, "But it was only a word," is simply to rub salt in the wound. Benedict was perceptive when his ninth rule for humility spoke of keeping the tongue from evil. One's tongue and inappropriate words can create of lot of damage. In his "Tools for Good Works," Benedict counsels his monks: "Guard your lips from harmful or deceptive speech" (RB 4.51).

Benedict recognized that respect makes special demands of leaders. For them, a process of discernment is a constant need. Discernment, or *discretio*, as Benedict named it, was essential in making the best decision possible in the circumstances. From an emotional intelligence perspective, discernment is the fruit of flexibility (FL), the result of recognizing concrete circumstances and knowing how to adapt to changing circumstances.

Benedict shapes his understanding of discernment by reminding the leader not only that he must be prudent, but also that he "always be wary of his own brittleness" and "not to break the bent reed" (RB 64.13). Even in correcting someone, or applying discipline, an abbot must "not overdo it" (RB 64.12). Why? Benedict is down to earth: "If [the abbot] is too vigorous in removing the rust, he may break the vessel." How many managers realize that insight … but after the fact, giving truth to the dictum that employees don't leave organizations, they leave managers.

Patience: Benedict saw patience as a necessity for any community. This meant that members "should bear each other's weaknesses of both body and character with the utmost patience" (RB 72.5). This is a tall order: not merely to endure the foibles and weaknesses of others, but to live with them and to help lift them with their burdens. A quick glance at our workplace tells us how heavy the demand of carrying others' burdens can be. Not only do we have our personal burdens to bear, but the task can be especially difficult in the workplace because of the many other pressures there.

The question, then, becomes "How can we carry others' burdens when we have enough worries of our own (physical, psychological, etc.) to take care of?" The Latin word *patientia* carries the idea of 'bearing under the weight of' or 'enduring,' or even 'suffering.' Today's dictionaries retain this sense, referring to "the quality of being patient, as the bearing of provocation, annoyance, misfortune, or pain, without complaint, loss of temper, irritation, or the like."[2] Being *im*patient means that one does not tolerate any discomfort, which leads to far more reactions than responses, the latter being the thought-out strategies in a situation vs. the reactive emotional outbursts.

In this author's experience, in scientific testing with the EQ-i™, the emotional competency known as Impulse Control (IC) is most often the lowest group factor; people react too quickly and often without reflection. Aristotle once remarked in his *Nichomachean Ethics*: "Anyone can become angry – that is easy. But to be angry with the right person, to the right degree, at the right time, for the right purpose, and in the right way – that is not easy" (Book II, 1109.a27).

Even apart from things like anger, today's onslaught of instant technologies, from email to cell phones and texting, makes it easy to recognize a wider patience problem. Benedict's critique of such an impatient world shows that it leaves little room for reflection – stillness – and that it requires a paradigm shift from external and quantitative values to internal and qualitative ones. On the positive side, Benedict reassures his monks that when one's heart accepts patience, a major step occurs – knowing oneself as one truly is. Each of us knows only too well that life provides us with ongoing opportunities to practise patience; the challenge is to see them not always as impositions, but as assets that builds both community and self.

Openness: Often today, people fail to see the value in what Benedict calls "order," that there is a definite way to do things. But for Benedict, right order was neither bureaucratic nor authoritarian. It was instead at the service of civility and respect, of being in community so that the inner call to wholeness could grow and mature. Rules for rules' sake were not Benedictine. He always called his *Rule* a "modest rule" (RB 73.8) outlining the path to wholeness, regardless of rank, age or seniority. This path to wholeness was always a journey of openness, to others and to all things.

'Openness' and 'revelation' are very different things. Openness is a here-and-now quality, a response to a situation, person or challenge. Revelation is exposing the parts of ourselves – feelings, opinions, and so on – that we would share with a best friend or a mentor. While revelation should be exercised only with discretion, openness is an ongoing necessity, since it applies precision of specific thinking and feeling to immediate events. In the community called the workplace, employees and managers alike should be expected to be open. They should be expected to speak their minds (and hearts) on what is under discussion. Not to do so can only open the door to misunderstanding. Still, the notion of specific thinking and feeling is more challenging than most people would assume, since it means crafting one's thoughts well and never as simple reactions, and always without attributing negative things to others.

Benedict's conditions are certainly challenging. Keep in mind that when he employs the notion of 'openness,' he uses the word *obœdientia*, or 'obedience.' This word frightens many people, but when seen through Benedict's eyes, it is not simply a military-style demand, but rather a deep listening to one's context. The Second Vatican Council, in its document on "The Church in the Modern World," said that Christians must truly listen to "the signs of the times."[3] This is obedience in a profound sense: being open to God's surprises in our lives. When we understand that such interruptions, however sudden or dramatic, can have meaning, we begin to listen to the beat of a different drummer. Being open in that sense is always a challenge because we know, on some level, that such unexpected interruptions can change our lives, making us rethink ourselves and our chosen pathways.

Within the workplace, as with life in general, change can often bring emotional pain and discomfort, but it is frequently the lack of empathy on the part of leaders when employees are working their way through such change that creates toxicity. Benedict foresaw these kinds of problems. His notion of community and openness was not only lateral, as between fellow workers, but vertical as well, from the top down and from the bottom up.

Still, the one thing that Benedict knew would gut a community was what he called *grumbling* or *murmuring*.[4] Grumbling was a spoken – but more often an unspoken and internal – complaining about one's situation. Community had no place for such grumbling: "Above all, the evil of murmuring must not appear for any cause by any word or gesture whatsoever" (RB 34.6). Even when it was internal, such complaining created nothing less than organizational toxicity, if for no other reason than it diminished the transparency that openness requires.

Action: Benedict doesn't expect community to be based on just nice words or feel-good sentiments. Being emotionally intelligent is not about being nice, either. He sees building community as a call to action, to the performance of good works or "virtuous living" (RB 21.4). Only this can implement what would otherwise remain simply an ideal. Action makes the foundation of community a solid one. Even the very first word of his *Rule*, "Listen," does not imply a passive subject. It is instead a call to action, to be attentive to what one hears. Benedict reminds his monks that when they have truly listened, it will be evident because of their follow-through actions (RB 39).

Benedict assumes that even "impossible tasks" (RB 68), when done in a spirit of community respect, patience and openness, will be growth opportunities for both the individual and the community as a whole. But even when it comes to simple daily tasks, each one must put into practice the community vision of work, which always embraced a higher purpose. Benedict always saw action as coming from an inner vision, and not just something instrumental to deal with the immediate situation.

For Benedict, the action that builds community, especially on the part of leaders, is not just a matter of encouraging words. It had to be accompanied by example and modelling, above all "for those who are recalcitrant or naïve" (RB 2.12), that is, modelling behaviour for those who are emotionally closed and immature. One is found to be "superior" or "better than others" only through "good works" and by being humble (RB 2:21) – bearing in mind that humility means that the person is down to earth, a real person dealing with real situations and real feelings (not one who comes across as plastic or hollow). Action always means "Show me the money!" For Benedict, this is one's job description. Just desiring to act appropriately is not enough.

For Benedict, therefore, work is certainly to serve God, but it is clear that work is also for the good of the self, the community and the wider society. Nevertheless, to fully develop the vision of work as a communitarian one is often a tall order. Still, some organizations today consciously aim for excellence in this area, recognizing that real collaboration not only respects the individual workers but enhances organizational productivity and innovation. Philosopher Alisdair McIntyre's words when he acknowledged Benedict's ability to speak to a contemporary world underline in particular his *Rule*'s emphasis on community: "What matters at this stage is the construction of local forms of community within which civility and the intellectual and moral life can be sustained."[5]

A Benedictine approach to work teaches us not only that work is our gift to the world, our social fruitfulness, but that such work is always done as a common effort, in community. The historian of work, Herbert Applebaum, has observed the practical effects of this approach: "The Benedictine system demonstrated how efficiently daily work could be done when it was collectively planned and ordered, when there was cooperation rather than coercion, and when the whole [person] was employed."[6]

Moreover, the community itself grows and derives excellence from working together, for work allows us to focus on someone or something besides ourselves, and in that way draws us away from self-centredness and toward 'otherness.' Benedict was a true egalitarian when it came to work. In his communities, those who entered became 'brothers' to one another ('sisters' in female communities); even former slaves were given such respect. The equal obligation for all to work built community among very diverse persons. In living in this self-forgetful manner, one does become self-fulfilled, but one also contributes to others. Benedict links working and purpose; work becomes *worth*while. For Benedict, both the spiritual and the physical journey of life was always one taken "together" (RB 72.12) – every action, including work, builds community as it advances. The most recent research would agree. In terms of the job satisfaction level of employees, organizational values and a sense of community consistently rank as the most important values. Benedict would be thrilled, but concerned to see that these too-often neglected values would be recognized in practice. 'Walking the talk' is essential for Benedict.

3

THE GOLDEN RULE: THE DIGNITY OF OUR COLLEAGUES

Remember the Golden Rule? 'Treat people as you would like to be treated.' The best managers break the Golden Rule every day. They would say don't treat people as you would like to be treated. This presupposes that everyone breathes the same psychological oxygen as you.
For example, if you are competitive, everyone must be similarly competitive. If you like to be praised in public, everyone else must, too. Everyone must share your hatred of micromanagement.

—Marcus Buckingham and Curt Coffman, Gallup[1]

While Buckingham and Coffman's quote outwardly seems to advocate breaking the traditional Golden Rule, their words actually capture its spirit: treat other individuals in the workplace in accord with their particular needs. We have seen that by its nature, work is communal. Even when one works alone, one is working in the end for the broader society and for a higher purpose. For Benedict, the community nature of work – and life –was something that must constantly be kept in mind and promoted. Yet he understood that community is a derived notion, something that is always composed of individuals. Respect for both the common good and the individual was a constant part of Benedict's balanced approach.

How do we develop this kind of wisdom for our own work life so we can respect both the whole community effort and, at the same time, each individual involved in it? Benedict didn't leave us without any clues. His *Rule* provides twelve concrete tips that enable us to navigate both the ordinary workday and the extraordinary situations we sometimes face.[2]

TIP #1: Accept that staying unconscious or unaware is too high a price to pay. Most of us would agree that falling in love is a very pleasant and enjoyable 'psychosis' (unconsciousness). But it has its other side; the inherent danger is that one ends up living out of the psychological pocket of the other person. This becomes what psychologists call enmeshment. The romantic mythology of 'two hearts beating as one' can be very costly: it is a mythology that is both addictive and not filled with growth. We end up living according to the desires of what we think the other person wants us to be. We never become ourselves.

Benedict does not advocate subjection but humility, getting one's feet on the ground, facing the reality of who we are. Overdependence is one form of lack of consciousness. The other is total self-involvement. Benedict's notion of grounding oneself in reality implies getting one's priorities straight, dropping the hubris, the swelled head and seriously egocentric thinking. This first step toward humility is a major one. Benedict gives us the image of a ladder – Jacob's ladder, to be exact (Gen. 28:12) – but the irony is that one goes 'up' by first going 'down' and learning about one's true place in life. This means realizing, in practice, that the universe doesn't revolve around us, that we're not its centre. Still, we have our place, and we need to appreciate that. Achieving balance often takes a lifetime, including many trials and many errors. The lesson is to be patient, and don't stop working at it.

TIP #2: Deal with your innate stubbornness in always wanting your own way. Such awareness often demands feedback from others. In organizations, this is often called 360° feedback. A CEO's refusal to encourage and listen to such feedback is known as 'CEO disease' – the vacuum around leadership when people withhold important information (most often, bad news). Emotionally intelligent leaders (and others at every level) actually *invite* negative feedback so they can be more and more realistic, more aware of what is going on.[3] Benedict would call this being more and more 'humble', renouncing a self-will that says, 'I am always right' (RB 7.31). Beginning to listen, both internally and externally, can greatly relieve our frustrations and prevent us from constantly knocking our head against a wall, not recognizing that there are ways around it. Theologian Reinhold Niebuhr (1892–1971) and his words come readily to mind: we can pray for the serenity to accept what we cannot change, the courage to change what we can, and the wisdom to know the difference. One CEO told me, after receiving anonymous corrective feedback that he had requested from his thirteen vice-presidents, "But I'm the president!" He implied that he should never receive negative feedback! We need to realize that we are not running the universe, and we don't have to be presidents to profit from feedback. Knowing better our strengths and weaknesses can not only be valuable self-knowledge, it can also make us more collaborative persons.

TIP #3: Accept that others have claims on and challenges to our commitments. We are not simply autonomous powers of control where our every wish is a command to others. This insight into our dependence on other individuals, on the broader society, and ultimately on the whole universe can be humbling. Still, Benedict constantly saw all life and work in this interconnected way. In 1992, then-president Bill Clinton remarked that what was needed was a "new covenant," implying that the issues of others and the environment were values that needed to be acknowledged.[4] We, too, must acknowledge the covenants and agreements that our relationships create. Some people may find awareness of this much easier in family situations than in work contexts. By the nature of work, however, not only our employer, but society and the wider universe have claims upon us. This applies to the entire workplace hierarchy. Bosses will always have bosses; no one is a "Supreme Leader." It is far more realistic – and personally helpful – when we don't act like one. It is also a way to respect the dignity of others.

TIP #4: Nurture the light rather than try to dispel the darkness. That means finding the kernel of truth and meaning, the positive, even in tough situations where emptiness seems all around. It is said that Mother Teresa (1910–1997) lived with 'inner darkness' – what is often called 'the dark night of the soul' – for 50 years. That is heroic. Each one of us has down times, moments where everything seems lost or going against us. Here, Benedict stresses perseverance, a shaft of light even in the routine (and sometimes drudgery) of living. Another Teresa, St. Teresa of Avila in Spain (1515–1582), once remarked that God is found among the pots and pans! The ordinariness of life! Obviously, this kind of perseverance and positive outlook demands emotional intelligence to help us deal with life's vicissitudes. Mentors and guides can be important, for they can help us see, even within ourselves and our immediate surroundings, what is not apparent in our own vision. Wise workplaces supply such mentorship, but even when they do not, the wisdom of colleagues, friends and family can offer helpful insight when things seem to be going wrong. Others may never tell us things we don't know, but they can help us to see things in perspective.

TIP #5: Learn when and how to drop the persona and just be ourselves. This means stopping the pretense that tells the world (and us) that we are other than we are. This is not to make public our psychological nakedness, but to cultivate a self-honesty that is more and more transparent to others around us. It means acknowledging that we have shortcomings; we have moral, psychological and spiritual 'warts.' None of us is perfect. Acting as if we are perfect is never helpful. One of the amazing results of Alcoholics Anonymous (AA) meetings, members say, is that their self-revelations are truly liberating – contrary to what they envisioned would happen when they first began to go to meetings. Pretending to be someone else is an exhausting job that rarely wins us points of any kind. We may be surprised at how much better our colleagues like the 'real' us, and not the plastic mask.

TIP #6: Learn to go with the flow. We often hear people say, "Give it a break!" They mean for the person to ease up, take it easy (or, at least, easier). There is something slightly ludicrous when we see on TV a multi-billionaire who is intent on making tens of millions more. Acquisitiveness is rampant in our society and it can be infectious. It has left many in our world trying to keep up. Besides burning themselves out, they are constantly on the consumer treadmill and feel they need the latest this and that.[5] We live in an age of extreme entitlement; a consumerist media does not help matters. It's true that we need certain things (food, shelter, etc.), but our society has turned many of our wants into needs. Benedict is adamant in his *Rule* that we must not confuse the two. He didn't say it in so many words, but he would be all in favour of taking the time to smell the roses. Being at ease within ourselves is a great help toward easing our relationships with others.

TIP #7: Make a relationship with your shadow … and deal with it! When such a task is not dealt with, our shadow sides, especially the negative parts of ourselves, become like hot potatoes. We toss them and project them onto others. Then not only is the other seen as 'the enemy', but also we feel that we don't have to deal with our shadows. However, our impatience and frustration often give us away. It's our shadow tapping, trying to tell us something, but we won't listen and accept that tapping. We say instead, "It's that driver in front of me!" As Pogo said, "I have met the enemy and it is I!" Shakespeare said it in *Hamlet* when the title character recognized those who "doth protest too much" – a protestation that betrays and exposes their doubts. One valuable tip on being aware and recognizing a shadow projection is this: "What I see in other people is more-or-less correct if it only *informs* but it is definitely a projection if it strongly *affects* me emotionally."[6] If you find that you are overly attached to or dependent on someone, this is called *shadow-hugging*; if you are feeling overly hateful, angry, frustrated with someone and always in conflict, this is called *shadow-boxing*.[7] Benedict's insight here says that once we become aware of our own shadow selves, we stand a better chance of accepting the foibles of others and empathizing with them. Most workplaces are home to many and varied characters. We need to see ourselves as one of them.

TIP #8: Honour a trusted and shared value path. Benedict tells us that we don't have all the answers; we are not God. That is true of life in general; it is obviously true of any workplace situation. Margaret Wheatley, an American management consultant and writer, says that relationships make our context – assuming, of course, that such relationships are healthy.[8] Healthy relationships and their trusted values are the communities we need in order to grow. We need others, and in the workplace we need others' wisdom and collaboration. A healthy workplace is not filled with codependent individuals, but with people who are vibrant, alive. Questions such as "Who are the wise people among us?" and "Where is wisdom found?" need to be asked by each of us, especially in difficult situations.

TIP #9: Talk less, listen more. This is Benedict personified. We are often in such a rush to get our own point across that we fail to listen to the other person, let alone grasp what they are communicating. To think that the other person does not realize we're not listening is an illusion. We would be surprised how strong is the awareness of non-communication; we have almost certainly experienced it ourselves. Actually, it's interesting to experience how much communication occurs in communities that practise silence. Such a statement today probably sounds strange in our culture, which encourages people to get in the last word. Benedict constantly encouraged discretion in speech. We could ask: "What I am going to say? Will it improve on the silence?" Rather than answering the other's point, it is often better to say, "Did I hear you say that you were thinking …?" Like everything else in the *Rule*, Benedict's virtue of balance is always called for.

TIP #10: Don't ridicule others; be straight. We sometimes hear the expression "But I was only joking!" in response to someone who has felt hurt or been embarrassed by us. Why do we say this? Because we feel uncomfortable as well and don't want to make an apology. Words and ridicule hurt. Kidding can be a cruel form of getting even or of discrimination. Making fun of other people, even when we think we are only playing and our colleague should just toughen up, is wrong. Healthy laughter is fine. According to a Chinese saying, "Beware of the person whose belly does not move when they laugh!" Inappropriate laughter often creates immediate hurt and ongoing interpersonal suspicion. Can the other person truly laugh with us? If not, we lack the respect that we would want for ourselves.

TIP #11: Grow peace, not discord. As we're "working the steps," as AA would say, we learn the important ascetical and ethical practice of 'using inner voice.' This can tell us that sometimes it is important just to remain silent. On cherishing silence, Benedict quotes from the Book of Proverbs: "The tongue holds the key to life and death" (RB 6.5). How many times have people said that they wished they had kept quiet rather than blurting out something? In certain situations, keeping to our inner voice is essential. This inner voice is not mysterious, but something inside us that speaks loudly if we take the time to listen. It can guide us to be peacemakers and facilitators rather than people who sow division. Benedict tells us that gentleness is a value worth cultivating. The wise person speaks "few words" (RB 7. 61) – that is, the choice of words is pertinent and measured, a sign of empathy and respect for the other person, even when the two of you disagree about the issue. Benedict's message applies as much to the workplace today as it did to his monastery in the sixth century.

TIP #12: Manifest serenity. Realize, as Carl Jung pointed out, that the inner and the outer are the same, that as within, so it is without. With this realization, a fuller sense of personhood emerges; a more whole person is born. This state, of course, is never static or forever, but is constantly being renewed. A deep sense of simplicity shows itself; it is this quality, with its serenity, that is so attractive to others. A person with obvious internal conflict is hardly a helpful problem solver at any level. While we should never be complacent with our spiritual journey, we realize at some point what Benedict promised in his *Prologue*: that our heart will overflow with "the inexpressible delight of love" (v. 49). Such inner calm is not only helpful to the self; it allows us to better appreciate the feelings of others around us.

Taken together, these Benedictine tips – Benedict's twelve steps of humility – create for us a path: a path for life itself and for our work life, where relationships become intense and surprisingly intimate. It is a path that values both self-worth and respect for others, a path that needs to become habitual in thinking (head) and in loving (heart). It is through such respect – what we envision as the Golden Rule – that we find wisdom, "the greatest human capacity according to some of the most prolific thinkers in history including King Solomon, Confucius, Socrates, Plato, Aristotle, and Thomas Aquinas."[9] To this list, we would add Benedict and his *Rule*.

4

ENLIGHTENED LEADERSHIP AND DECISION MAKING

Leadership is always dependent on the context,
but the context is established by the relationships we value.

—Margaret Wheatley, *Leadership and the New Science*[1]

The purpose of leadership is to create context. We have seen how important connectedness is to the creating, framing, sharing and sustaining of context. The idea of context was Benedict's main purpose in writing and living his *Rule*. Above all, he wanted his monks to become aware of the divine presence in community, as in all things. Listening was central to this task of leadership because of the subtleties involved in hearing God's voice among the chatter and clamour of everyday activities. Today, as in Benedict's time, his leadership message and context for decision making were counter-cultural: the need for leadership wisdom in the face of the intense pull of pragmatism.

LEADERSHIP-WISDOM

In taking Benedict and his *Rule* as our guide to leadership and decision making, I intend to emphasize its consistency of vision. Contemporary research has drawn attention to something that Benedict would have cherished: the critical role of wisdom in the thinking and feeling needed for leadership. Great scholars have seen wisdom as the highest human capacity, the most noble and worthy of human pursuits. Aristotle argued that wisdom began in wonder or in asking questions. Benedict would have been quite concerned that the emphasis on leadership today has often adopted a decidedly more quantitative and competitive focus. Organizational profits and efficiencies have taken a front-row-centre spot. Benedict would reject neither, since he saw production and excellence as vital to the support and quality of the life of the monastery, but he saw both of these as secondary – the product, not the source, of enlightened leadership. Although business schools and MBA programs foster and support a focus on outcomes, such a vision is doomed from the beginning, since it neglects leadership's essential qualities.

For Benedict, leadership and wisdom go hand in hand. Benedict's abbot leads by example. His authority is exercised wisely by serving others first, not by self-aggrandizement (RB 64.8), invoking mercy over judgment, acting prudently and avoiding extremes (RB 64.9). For leaders, discernment is "the mother of all virtues" (RB 64.19). Such wisdom would allow the strong to feel challenged and the weak encouraged (RB 64.19). Benedict connects "wisdom in teaching" as one of the necessary criteria in the election of a leader-abbot (RB 64.2). Most of us have had the experience of wisdom-leaders on our life's journey; they not only spoke the right word (head, ethics), they also touched us deeply (heart, value). They were able to combine the emotional with the intellectual, values and actions.

If wisdom is so primary and so essential to leadership, we need to understand some caveats before embarking on decision making if we are going to pursue and develop it. First, we must beware of leaders who are false prophets, pretending to be wise, but whose lives foster toxic relationships. You will be able to recognize true leaders "by their fruits": caring, joy, peace, patience, kindness, goodness, faithfulness, self-control, reasonableness, compassion, impartiality and sincerity. Most employees can intuitively sense judicious leadership from the leader's way of acting.

Second, given widespread employee disengagement, leaders must become aware of the importance of the common good. Much of to-day's leadership wisdom is myopic and dehumanizing. An emphasis on a *commodity-based vision* geared toward efficiencies and profits completely overlooks employee well-being, the common good and the longer-term benefits – a *meaning-based vision*.[2] An abbot-leader thinks of others before himself (RB 64.8), balancing and integrating doing *right* (ethics) and doing *good* (values) in thinking and action. Leadership wisdom keeps in focus the common good: that of the employees, the company and the society that the company serves, and not the benefit to the leader himself or herself.

Third, leaders must acknowledge what is often called the "fear of foolishness," that is, the fear of appearing foolish in other people's eyes.[3] St. Paul captured this leadership idea in one of his letters to the Corinthians: "We are fools for the sake of Christ" (1 Cor. 4:10) – in other words, we are seen to be at odds with prevailing standards. But recognizing that we should not tailor our thoughts to the acceptance of others also involves a respect for what at first may seem to be foolishness on others' part, for this may prove not to be the case. Wisdom leaders are sensitive to Benedict's insight on participative community decision making that required every member to attend, since matters under discussion affect everyone. Here, the leader knows not to ignore or dismiss a younger member because they may have an insight that is new (RB 3.3). The expression that "fools rush in where angels fear to tread" is apt here because being constrained by a fear of foolishness creates moral, psychological, emotional and spiritual blindness in the leader. Further, the impression that a leader is closed to suggestions that are entirely novel or would entail major change is one of the great barriers to innovation.

A wholesome fear of foolishness accords well with the Benedictine notions of humility, simplicity and transparency. Moreover, it means that leaders realize they don't have all the answers for the common good of their stakeholders, and opens them to new possibilities. In other words, the fear of foolishness is double-edged: from a positive perspective, a leader is not afraid to embrace foolishness, that is, fear of being considered foolish, when the situation involves key human values that need to be honoured but that others may consider 'silly' or foolish. From a negative perspective, a 'foolish' leader – or a leader without a sense of wisdom – simply charges ahead, ignoring the signals and feelings and intuitions that caution him/her in making certain decisions not only because they have rejected any feelings of possibly looking foolish to those around them, but also because winning at all costs for increased shareholder value drives them on without respect to the dignity and worth of employees and the community and environment within which the company is situated. The case of Enron Corp. is a classic example of this negative aspect of ignoring the fear of foolishness in action. Senior executives simply did not care what impact their decisions had on employees.

Some authors interpret this latter sense of the fear of foolishness as the avoidance of foolishness, but the more proper word here would be recklessness, which ultimately stems from a leader's egocentrism or assumed omniscience. This often leads to an unrealistic optimism that allows leaders-without-wisdom to believe they are smarter than others and can do what they want. It can also lead to an inflated sense of power, where others are seen as mere mortals. Or it can lead to a sense of invulnerability, as if no one will ever hold them accountable for their actions. It goes without saying that the literature harshly describes such leaders as functionally stupid.[4] An amazing caution to this idea of being *functionally stupid* because people see themselves as better than others comes from St. Paul: "Don't fool yourself. Don't think that you can be wise merely by being up-to-date with the times. ... What the world calls smart, God calls stupid. It's written in Scripture, '... The Master sees through the smoke screens of the know-it-alls" (1 Cor. 3:18-19).[5]

The *final* caveat is a general, overriding one. Above all, there must be trust. Research over the years has shown that authority has four pivot points: authority by *position*, authority by *knowledge*, authority by *behaviour*, and authority by *trust*.[6] If trust is lacking, the other three factors carry little or no credibility for followers. Trust is essential. One has only to look at the military for an example: without trust in superior officers, the whole chain of command collapses. Benedict understood this principle. He says that the abbot must "always remember" who he is: he has much to account for (RB 2.30) because much has been entrusted to him. In other words, he holds much *in* trust. We all have examples of leaders we could not trust. We can say that without trust, even with the other three factors present, leadership is weak or missing. Such leaders try to compensate by overemphasizing their intelligence or position – which only goes to showcase their arrogance and ends up diminishing their authority.

A paradigm shift for today's leaders and managers may be difficult. All change has its challenges. But change is a double-edged sword: while it cuts away old stuff, cutting prunes so that new growth becomes possible. Wisdom is a means to let the truth flourish; wise leaders empower their workplaces to let this happen.

RE-VISIONING PRACTICAL DECISION MAKING

Briefly, to be a leader in Benedict's vision meant a different set of priorities, a re-visioning of tried-and-true notions, such as what constitutes strength, power, fullness and success. In such a re-visioning, leadership wisdom contextualizes decision making as 'practical wisdom': *knowing* what is the ultimate good, *doing* what is right, and integrating these two factors to arrive at the best decision for the common good. Although Benedict doesn't use the term 'practical wisdom,' it is clear in his *Rule* that wisdom is inherently linked to human behaviour and relationships – the *what* as well as the *who*. For Benedict, prudence and kindness go together: the leader is able to discern when direction is just enough and not too much. Practical wisdom leadership requires not only a leader who has grown in matters of self-actualization, but who has also moved *beyond* this to self-transcendence, to seeking meaning beyond personal and corporate self-interests to interests involving the wider common good.

Research names several "red flags" that leaders always face in decision-making situations. These are the subtle and not-so-subtle prejudices that warp reality, the faulty experiences carried over from previous situations, inappropriate self-interests, and personal attachments to past decision contexts that distort current circumstances. Dealing with these red flags demands interiority and self-reflection.

What are some common unconscious and pre-conscious routines that trap or block a leader in making good decisions? Research on leadership decision making identifies at least eight major ones (see Table 1).[7]

TABLE 1: PSYCHOLOGICAL TRAPS OR UNCONSCIOUS
ROUTINES WHEN MAKING DECISIONS

EIGHT PSYCHOLOGICAL TRAPS IN DECISION MAKING: BECOMING MORE CONSCIOUS OF UNCONSCIOUS ROUTINES		
NUMBER	**TRAP**	**EXPLANATION**
1	ANCHORING	Initial or first impressions and information having an inordinate influence on future decisions. "Decision making by blinkers!" We get a 'fix' on an experience that then guides and selects new information. The result? A leader with tunnel vision. New information or possibilities offer little interest. "My mind's made up!" What is deemed not to fit is screened out. A leader gets 'stuck in a groove.'
2	STATUS QUO	Here the leader's motto becomes 'don't rock the boat.' Some might say he or she fears change, even when the change appears advantageous. Risk is bad! Change is scary! Tradition trumps creativity and innovation. The workplace often becomes a place of 'groupthink,' a type of 'intellectual communism.'
3	SUNK COST	Reluctance to admit making a mistake and trying to justify past decisions. For example, throwing good money after bad. Such a leader is afraid to 'clear the plate,' so to speak, make new choices and start afresh irrespective of past 'costs' or mistakes. Reluctance to 'suck it up' and get on with things.
4	CONFIRMING-EVIDENCE	Going with data that creates a self-fulfilling prophecy that does not allow for contradictory evidence. Such a trap is the 'motherlode' for a leader to use abusive power in decision making. Associates sense the leader's mind is already made up and feel there's no sense in arguing. The leader says, "Don't bother me with the evidence!"

5	FRAMING	Depending on how a leader "frames" the context structures the kind of decision to be made. A leader may frame a potential decision in terms of past experience (an anchoring trap frame) or frame it around a lost opportunity (a sunk-cost frame). It all depends on perspective: is the glass half-full or is the glass half-empty?
6	OVERCONFIDENCE	A leader unrealistically inflates projections (±) or outcomes – an Icarus strategy from mythology. With waxen wings, Icarus flew too close to the sun, so that the wings melted and he fell into the sea. This reflects not only unreality but also an egocentrism that excludes the wisdom of others. It can also illustrate the recklessness that happens from ignoring the fear of appearing foolish.
7	OVERCAUTION	Being overly cautious and playing it safe. There is a constant stalling in making a decision; important decisions are postponed, sort of a managerial 'waiting for Godot' situation where nothing occurs. The leader remains 'frozen' in front of circumstances, sitting and never getting off the proverbial pot!
8	RECALLABILITY	Knowledge of a past dramatic or overwhelming event that blocks a leader from moving on and making new decisions. The tragedy of 9/11 left deep impressions on many people. Does that mean that one shouldn't fly anymore? Being unduly influenced by the last person you spoke to can be an example also of such a block. The latest dramatic news can be very persuasive and unconsciously 'drive' us in our decision making.

Much of the influence of Benedict and his *Rule* over the centuries was due to his appreciation of wisdom leadership and how it could frame and support the decisions people would need to make. He knew that a good leader had to be a wise leader, attuned to the common good and able to see beyond the immediate moment. Good contemporary psychology teaches us to recognize the 'functional stupidity'[8] that organizations often support because they trivialize a necessary paradigm shift that is needed to change from a kind of intellectual positivism, or numbers game to increase shareholder value only, over reflectiveness and the development of interiority. Decision traps and the inordinate fear of foolishness literally 'trap' unwise leaders in their pursuit of short-term gains over what they believe will be unnecessary long-term rewards – if at all. Truly, a revolution of the imagination is needed.

5

THE ART OF LISTENING: THE NEW OBEDIENCE

We have two ears and one mouth,
so we should listen more than we speak.

—Zeno of Citium, as quoted by Diogenes

The *Rule of Benedict* could easily be called *The Book of Listening*. "Listen" is his first word, and its spirit pervades everything he wrote. A world that so often seems to be moving on a treadmill sorely needs listening skills. We saw earlier that genuine listening involves two things: *understanding* the other and *accepting* the other. The Chinese character for 'intense listening' can be very helpful here:

Ears · Eyes · Undivided Attention · Heart

Figure 1: Chinese character for listening

Listening takes time and effort. As the Chinese character suggests, we listen not only with our ears. We also listen with our eyes – the windows of the soul, as they have been called – and with our heart (in Benedict's words, "the ear of your heart"). This takes effort: undivided attention, in the sense of 'attending to.' It is something we do consciously and deliberately. We now realize that admonitions from primary school teachers to 'sit up and pay attention' have more meaning than we originally thought!

The art of listening demands both a certain quality of and time for silence. Silence does not lie. Silence zeroes in on one's inner world, its chaos and its life-giving prescriptions – what the early monastic tradition called 'thoughts.' It was essential that disordered desires at the root of 'thoughts' – eight of which Evagrius Ponticus (345–399), a Christian monk and ascetic from Egypt, first called *logismoi* in Greek and then systematized – be confronted and controlled because they could fire up the passions. Tradition after the thirteenth century has flagged them as the seven deadly sins: Lust, Gluttony, Greed, Sloth, Wrath, Envy and Pride. These early desert hermits and monks were clearly on to something important about human nature!

Many people today crave silence but rarely structure their time for silence to take the lead. Not being able to stand silence, they are telling the world that they cannot stand themselves, and then wonder why others find it difficult to be with them. There seems to be an unspoken or unconscious conspiracy against silence these past few years. What some people consider sound, others consider simply noise. People seem to be afraid of silence; hence, malls and homes have music or TV or some other sound going on all the time. The ever-present iPhones and headphones are constantly on, whether the person is walking down the street, sitting on the bus or subway, even having a family dinner out at a fast-food restaurant. We are inundated by noise.

Our world of silence grows our abilities to listen to others with eyes, ears and heart because we have attended to such silence within. Silence values *stillness*. In earlier centuries, a Russian monk could be called an 'urban hesychast' for "preserving inwardly a secret center of stillness in the midst of outward pressures, carrying the desert with us in our hearts wherever we go."[1] *Hesychasm* is the Greek word for 'stillness,' 'tranquility.' In effect, the urban hesychast was a person who, even amid the city's bustle and pressures, possessed an inner sense of stillness that gifted those around them. Perhaps we can encourage such a disposition in leaders and managers today so that in the midst of the pressures of work, inner and outer are more integrally balanced.

It may seem strange to say that first of all we need to listen to the silence. It is in listening to the silence that one begins to hear things besides the tyranny of external pressures and one's own current urges; rather, we begin to hear the voice of the transcendent and mystery within us. Dutch theologian Edward Schillebeeckx, O.P., wrote, "Although it is … impenetrable, a mystery does always have a nucleus of openness, of intelligibility."[2] It is this intelligibility that silence unveils. Mother Teresa said, "We need to find God, and he cannot be found in noise and restlessness. God is the friend of silence. See how nature – trees, flowers, grass – grows in silence; see the stars, the moon and the sun, how they move in silence."[3] Silence is not a void that must be filled; it is a friend with whom we can be totally at ease.

LISTENING AND ATTENTION

Listening involves an attending to, a giving over of oneself, a giving to beyond oneself. It is truly an ex-centric activity – the ability to stand outside our own self, our own personal concerns, as legitimate as they may be, and truly see the other. In this attending to the other, two movements take place: (1) understanding the other person (a cognitive, head dimension), and (2) showing empathy with the other person (an affective, heart dimension). Both dimensions are required. In other words, can I understand this person in what is being said or done, and can I appreciate this person just for being who they are? Can I listen by attending to these two movements and noticing what is happening? I remember a couple I was counselling many years ago. She kept saying to him, "But you never listen!" He would continually say, "But I do listen to you." What I finally realized was that she was asking for *empathy* as a true sign of his ability to listen. The chaff point was that he felt he did listen to her because he *understood* what she was trying to get at. Both were involved in the listening process … but only partially. The conundrum was resolved when I pointed out the two movements essential to listening: understanding and empathy.

His task was to expand his listening ability to include more of the heart dimension (empathy) and her task was to realize and become more aware that he was in fact listening to her but mainly from a cognitive perspective. Both agreed that they had to work through these growing pains.

As we have seen, any practice found in the *Rule* is always the result of an ongoing, deep personal self-examination – what I call 'an ecology of emotions.' The term suggests that just as we become more and more conscious of ecological matters around us in terms of our physical environment, Benedict's advice in his Chapter 4 on "The Tools for Good Works" is also an ecology: that of the emotions which, when such emotions are attended to more and more intelligently (a process we have seen that involves both cognitive or head and affective or heart disciplines), establishes a cleaner and clearer ground from which people can listen more effectively. This ecology includes first choosing a different way of acting from what society models for us – a society or world that Jesus has said he has "overcome" (John 16:33) and that we, too, can overcome. Such a victory is central to Benedict's vision for us to live a life *worth* living and to build a future *worth* going to.

An ecology of the emotions would provide awareness of a number of selected shadow issues: how anger influences and impacts a person, how grudges and revenge need to be quickly identified and eliminated, the importance and process of loving one's enemies, and dealing with perceived unjust treatment – to name a few (4.1-33). Benedict knew that one cannot listen, for example, with an angry heart. Modern psychology would back up his intuition: we cannot truly listen to another person, for example, if we do not like them. This can present a major problem if a manager must work with an employee he or she dislikes, or a parent must deal with a rebellious teenager! The solution, of course, is to find something of value about that other person: even, as Carl Jung said, to realize that however much we dislike the person and cannot right now listen to them, this other person has at least the right to exist. This value may be difficult for the listener to hold onto, and great discipline and practice of the art of listening are required. Such discipline in learning the art of listening is the demand of the "new obedience" that updates Benedict's intention "to establish a school" (P45), which his *Rule* wanted to put in place.

THE NEW OBEDIENCE

Benedict lays out his demands in terms of listening: factors like community, respect and patience, to name a few. Vatican II would add that we listen to the signs of the times, but this is really a further update of Benedict that would require attention and engagement with contemporary tools such as psychology and the vast array of social science skills. Today's 'new obedience' demands nothing less. With these new tools we learn little by little to listen not only to words, but also to their meaning. Often the meaning is hidden in the images a person uses. Carl Jung makes a remarkable comment that is so important to our own image of the art of listening: "To the extent that I managed to translate the emotions into images – that is to say, to find the images that were concealed in the emotions – I was inwardly calmed and reassured. Had I left those images hidden in the emotions, I might have been torn to pieces by them."[4]

While Jung is talking about his own emotions, we can easily extrapolate his wisdom and apply it to both parties: the listener and the person who wants to be listened to. Susan Rowland, a Jungian scholar, warns of the price we pay if we ignore emotionality: "Anything derived merely from rationality risks being profoundly inauthentic unless it also bears witness to the destabilizing presence of the unconscious."[5] In picking up on only the words, we miss out on the most difficult task; we must get beneath the words and discover their meaning. The art of listening demands that we listen also to the imagery and factors of meaning in the other person and mirror these pieces back for clearer understanding. Another way of saying this is that we must learn to 'read the white spaces' well in our conversations and not become locked into one 'anchored' experience and, therefore, an earlier situational meaning. Things change, and listening involves being open to hear the new (*conversatio morum*).

The description of listening as the new obedience is inherent even in the etymology of the words. True listening means to listen 'in the direction of' – which equates to the "*ob*" in the Latin *obœdientia*, a word that is composed of *ob* + *audire*, literally, to listen 'because of'. Obedience is one of three obligations – vows – to which Benedictine monks pledge themselves. It is a value that Benedict holds dearly, but never in a slavish manner. In its broader sense of the art of listening, we can readily transpose this concept to the workplace to bring about a greater sense of employee engagement. With real listening, the *acedia* or 'I-don't-give-a-damn' attitude that is disengagement could be minimized. This is especially important for effective leadership. In Benedict's terms, effective leaders become servant leaders: they stand firm (*stabilitas*) in their commitments to dignity and respect, they are open to feedback and change (*conversatio morum*), and they truly listen (*obœdientia*) both to the words and to the meanings of their colleagues.

In essence, *obœdientia* as the art of listening means that workers *appreciate* their colleagues because they value the other, give thanks for them and recognize their worth. Such attitudes (appreciation, valuing, gratitude and worth) are deeply involved in this kind of obedience since they are woven into the tapestry of true listening. People know if someone is listening to them or not. In examining why a person is not listening, one finds some of these four qualities and attitudes missing in the encounter. The problem that constantly gets in the way, especially for managers, is that of *power*. Managers are usually very clear about what they want or need for their organizations … or at least they think they know what they want and need. But clear-sightedness and decisiveness often translate into a lack of respect and appreciation, which in turn fosters an authoritarianism that precludes real listening.

Still, like all invitations to a paradigm shift, we have choices. Is it possible that leaders and managers can measure up to this new millennial demand for interiority, reflection and change in behaviour and priorities? From a commodity-based perspective, it's 'product, product, product'. From a meaning-based perspective, it's not only product, but also engaged employees who are passionate about what they do because they feel deeply appreciated and will go the extra mile, as Gallup points out.[6] Product is not excluded, but excellence, well-being and innovation also enter into the formula. Today, groups of engaged employees are relatively small compared to all the employees who could be engaged in their work. The potential for something quite different is enormous. One of the main differences lies in how managers and leaders practice the art of listening, or in embracing the new obedience. Personal change nearly always comes very slowly, but the options for change are always before us.

To summarize: real listening is an act of love and deep caring for the other, warts and all. The art of listening demands an obedience to being "ex-centric," the ability to step outside one's self-centredness or, as St. Catherine of Sienna (1347–1380) said, "the cloud of self-centredness." It involves not only seeing intellectually, but also with the heart. It means noticing that colleagues really want to be listened to. It takes an inner silence to ground this new paradigm shift, but that also gifts each of us with hope and confidence. Taken from the perspective of emotional intelligence, "attunement" becomes a wonderful word, since, in paying attention, we must be attuned to what is going on around us. To be 'aligned' has more to do with a logic, a set of priorities, whereas attunement draws on "diffuse awareness."[7] The demands of the new paradigm push each of us to make room for these new learnings: listening, communication and fluency in emotional intelligence skills. At a deeper level, we must recognize that the opaque in life is both necessary and magnificent, that things do not always have to be clear, and that mystery is embedded in the very fabric of the universe, including in ourselves and in others. As children, we were sometimes told to sit up straight and to make straight lines. Learning self-control is a value, of course, but life is never quite 'straight.' No lives are lived in a straight line. One woman in a counselling situation told me one time, "I never cry in a straight line!" Listening helps us and others untangle 'crooked lines' to help make them straighter. When that happens, we can breathe more confidently and effortlessly. Can there be a more important reason, personally and organizationally, for being obedient to the art of listening?

6

OPENNESS TO CREATIVITY: THE SPIRIT OF CURIOSITY

In a time of drastic change
it is the learners who inherit the future.
The learned usually find themselves equipped
to live in a world that no longer exists.

—Eric Hoffer, *Reflections on the Human Condition*

Declining innovation has become a major organizational problem as well as a serious symptom of employee disengagement. In almost every workplace, a major reality check is needed regarding the lack of openness to creativity, personally and organizationally. Gallup found that a great majority of engaged employees recognized that their colleagues' creativity spurred them on, and commented, "Engaged employees work with passion and feel a profound connection to their company. They drive innovation and move the organization forward."[1] In fact, organizational psychologist Claudia Heimer argued that innovation is closely connected to managing emotions and that the complexity of the business environment demanded nothing less.[2] The need appears to be for employees who are attuned to such recognized emotional skills as flexibility, reality testing, empathy, optimism and social responsibility.

Recognizing the place of emotions in life, work and community, the *Rule of Benedict* is perhaps one of the most creative and integrative pieces of writing of all time. While the word "innovation" is absent, the concept of innovation permeates its pages. Indeed, three of Benedict's central themes are foundational to any innovative situation. First is the insistence on what Benedict called *conversatio morum*, a constant openness to change and improvement. Then there is his emphasis on listening and communication, the basis for collaboration. Finally, and perhaps most important, is Benedict's overriding optic of transcendence, going beyond the self to take into account not only others, but the wider universe in all this entails.

BEING OPEN TO TRANSCEND

We don't often associate innovation with spirituality or the quality of transcendence, but organizational literature is beginning to make the connection.[3] Ultimately, of course, a lack of creativity results from the fear and refusal to be open to allowing life to emerge rather than always wanting to dominate and control everything, the refusal to recognize that we are part of something greater. Transcendence provides a different viewpoint. First there is the very general consideration that a workplace where employees have a sense of the transcendent will always look for 'something more,' that is, will always see that the well-being of the staff, the quality of work, and the products or services offered can be improved. Second, there is a sense of social responsibility: we are selling these products and offering these services to customers we value and for the benefit of a wider world. This cannot fail to raise questions not only of how we can make a better product, but how we can make a safer one, and how we can make one that is more ecologically responsible. Finally, a transcendent outlook will encourage managers and employees to think in terms of the biggest picture possible and to think outside of any narrow box. In very practical terms, this can enable a workforce to vision in terms not only of what they are doing now, but what the wider world's needs are, and what possibilities there are that can meet these needs. That is when true innovation becomes possible.

Modern society has come to recognize that spirituality or the quality of transcendence is not only the possession of religious believers. In its broadest terms, transcendence represents a desire to go beyond the self, the personal, or even beyond relationships, the interpersonal, and to be connected and attuned to all that is, what we could call the transpersonal. It involves the character of ultimacy, which people may interpret in different ways, but which, if recognized, has a profound influence upon how life is lived. Bringing this character to the workplace and seeing one's work as a spiritual calling means that the creative and innate force within that seizes us and drives us to become who we are meant to be must be put to work. Otherwise, we choose to keep living "in a spiritually dumb culture characterized by materialism, expediency, narrow self-centredness, lack of meaning and dearth of commitment."[4]

St. Augustine (354–430), in his *Confessions*, calls this inborn natural inclination for self-transcendence an innate disposition, the heart's natural yearning for God (I, 1). It could also be described in more secular terms as a person's natural tilt to 'something more.' This inherent instinct for the spiritual is at the same time a natural impulse for creativity. Its lack becomes a human shortfall. Without creativity, we develop a binary system of thinking and feeling where surprise is missing, conveniently ignoring the fact that the opaqueness of life doesn't always make everything crystal clear; diffuse awareness is often ridiculed, ignored, rejected or denied. Openness to possibility, and therefore to the creative, is how we will grow and become all that we are meant to be, or, in ultimate terms, cultivate the quality of transcendence that was so key to Benedict.

Through the willingness to listen to the questions that life and circumstances present us with at each and every moment, transcendence provides the key to openness and creativity. I am talking here about listening to questions of meaning that emerge not only from without, but also from within. Of course, it takes the courage to move beyond the superficial ideas that surround us every day. We sometimes forget that what lies beneath the surface is the life-giving ordinariness of true reality, not the plastic alternatives presented to us. We underrate what a former student of mine described as "the power of curiosity," a reflection of Aristotle's intuition that wonder is the beginning of wisdom.

Unfortunately, the disengaged employee is characterized by a lack of openness and is blocked from being creative. There may be organizational or contextual reasons for this blockage, but who we are – the calling to be open to creativity – is absolutely required for a person to be engaged in their work. Obviously, full responsibility need not lie only with the employee. Abusing an employee's dignity and then demanding high work results is a recipe for disaster, for then the employee's innate openness to creativity gets choked. The employee becomes a cog, a piece in the process of production, usually doing only the minimum. Not only does this create personal and health issues, but the organization is effectively deprived of the employee's real talents. Innovation requires more.

BEING OPEN TO COMMUNICATE

As we have seen, Margaret Wheatley has pointed out that a leader's primary responsibility is to the context of the workplace; however, the fibre of this context is a relational one. There must be an openness to create relationships. In a truly effective and creative *worth*place, human connectedness is primary, both with valuing the *forming* of relationships and the ongoing *performing* of tasks that stem from them (teamwork). The openness that transcendence can bring needs to be nourished and sustained in practice in the context of such a worthplace community.

For innovation, connectedness and relationships matter tremendously. Some inventions may be the product of a single mind, but most of them are the results of collaborative efforts, often over an extended period of time. It is in the interchange of ideas that seminal insights are honed and developed, wrinkles are ironed out, bugs are fixed and projects come to fruition. It is in that same kind of open interchange that the talents of many different sorts are allowed to flow together and to complement one another. And that takes precisely the kind of communication that Benedict advanced in his *Rule*, a listening based on genuine respect for the other. This was the case even when it accepted the other's weaknesses (RB 72.5), for when this was done realistically, it also accepted, by implication, the other's strengths. It was also a listening that was open. It left out no one, neither the young nor the immature, nor the older person with their incapacities. It recognized not just the bonds of community, but the fact that productive ideas might come from any source (RB 3.3).

Openness, by its nature, means that we are able to put aside our own concerns, a posture that Benedict calls *humility*: the ability to step aside and not be the centre of attention. It is interesting that, along with intellectual arrogance, the most frequent block to openness in listening is fear. Benedict recognized the fear factor as a natural re-action, but counselled that one should not be daunted by it (P48). A spirit of openness to creativity means that we should never be afraid to ask questions, nor should we be afraid to let others question us. It is in the process of such dialogue that innovation best takes place. We saw how leaders with emotional intelligence ask for feedback, even negative feedback, because it's often typical that employees want to keep the bad news from the boss. Besides being unhealthy, this practice impairs the spirituality of cultivating organizational and employee questions: not just question-box ones, but real questions. Not being open to feedback fosters the creation of the negative organizational shadow or culture of secrecy that ultimately affects not only creativity but productivity.

As the 21st century began, manufacturing was far less important than in the previous century, and the service sector had grown to include some four out of five North American workers. Even more than before, this shift required the cultivation of interpersonal skills, innovation, teamwork, customer responsiveness, flexibility and the need for workers to cope with change by learning and unlearning. Moral philosopher Eric Hoffer reminded us in the opening quote to this chapter that in rapidly changing times, it is learners who will in-herit the future, and that the supposedly learned are well equipped only for a world that has disappeared. He prefaced that observation with a larger one, noting that education's central task was to "implant a will and a facility for learning" so that "learning people" would develop. A truly "learning society" was an ongoing and shared learning journey when "grandparents, parents, and children are students together."

Here Hoffer was almost directly echoing Benedict, who envisaged his community as an ongoing school and, like Hoffer, a school with no specific instructors. Within the Benedictine model, each person became a teacher to the other. Given the rapidly shifting needs of the workplace, the growth and development of the 'learning organization' became a paramount theme, but this often turned into a structured experience that underestimated the contribution to real learning that the daily open interaction and communication among employees was capable of providing. A spirituality of learning would take the notion of the learning organization a step further and begin pondering and anticipating how a *yearning* organization might develop.[5] Such a yearning organization would bring to consciousness the employees' need for the 'something more' that we have explored. The special role of leadership here would be to open up and encourage conversation. Emotional intelligence (EQ) would obviously be actualized in the yearning organization. I have always described EQ as the start of a conversation.[6] Peter Frost was perceptive when he wrote that "properly supported … employees will often contribute innovative solutions to problems, even when they lack the formal training to address them."[7] Benedict knew this. For him, work, mutual learning and creativity went together. Work was an activity of co-creation.

BEING OPEN TO CHANGE

Central to Benedict was his insistence on *conversatio morum*, the need for ongoing conversion and change. We drop old attitudes, behaviours and perceptions and open up to new possibilities. Moreover, that openness to change must be holistic, at one and the same time personal, professional and institutional. My colleague Michael Cox and I wrote in *The Seven Pillars of Visionary Leadership*,

> Only by undertaking a personal revolution of the imagination can we begin our journey to individual, organizational and community transformation. We need to leave behind the skewed value path that celebrated the separation of work and

well-being and re-create a culture in which imagination, innovation, learning and mastery of work are perceived as labours of love. We need to shift our thinking and find new ways to authenticate individual self-worth in the new organizational age. Only by freeing our imaginations can we loose the spirit of enterprise we need to build people, pride, and profits.[8]

This spirit of broad, ongoing change is thoroughly Benedictine; it is also foundational to creativity and innovation. In Benedict's terms, it affected both a way of doing things and a way of living. It involved not just the reluctant acceptance of change, but a spirit that recognized that change was a necessary factor of life itself. Moreover, it was an ongoing, lifelong process. There was never a sense of "Now that we've got here, it's time to take a break." At the same time, Benedict recognized that true change, the genuine alteration of attitudes and behavioural patterns, did not come in earthshaking flashes, but was incremental and slow moving; it took place in the context of daily life and interactions. And while change was expected, positive change was always the result of both personal and community assessment. Finally, there was a clear recognition on Benedict's part that change in attitude and actions did not take place in separate compartments, but very much went together.

Benedict recognized that openness to change was not only vital personally, but was essential if any community was to be a living one and not moribund. In workplace terms, such a spirit – like everything Benedictine, properly balanced – can transpose a static environment into a lively and creative one where new ideas are not only permitted but encouraged and welcomed. In effect, such an organization transforms itself institutionally through the liveliness and interest of the individuals who compose it. With that spirit of openness to change, innovation, both small and great, is almost certain to be a constant; without it, any organization is likely to be left behind.

7

THE PURSUIT
OF EXCELLENCE:
BUILDING WORTH

If it falls to your lot to be a street sweeper, go on out and sweep streets like Michelangelo painted pictures, sweep streets like Handel and Beethoven composed music, sweep streets like Shakespeare wrote poetry. Sweep streets so well that all the hosts of heaven and earth will have to pause and say, "Here lived a great street sweeper who did his job well."

—Martin Luther King Jr.,
New Covenant Baptist Church, Chicago, 1967

When IBM began, it was recognized for its hallmark of excellence. This was an organization that utilized the great energies of its people and what its founder, Thomas Watson, Jr. called the 'beliefs' it held for its employees. In fact, a best-selling book of the 1980s, *In Search of Excellence*, by Thomas J. Peters and Robert H. Waterman, found that truly excellent companies were characterized by well-defined sets of beliefs that guided them. Indeed, companies that had a very focused idea of their earnings per share and their financial objectives fared less well than the outstanding companies that had sets of guiding beliefs. Obviously, excellence came through a strong central value system, usually with beliefs such as the following – a laundry list that Benedict would have been proud of:

1. To be the best.
2. To follow through.
3. To recognize individuals.
4. To offer quality and service.
5. To take risks and support failure.
6. To communicate in a personal (read: 'engaged') way.
7. To recognize growth and rewards.

These are certainly some of the marks we would want to have associated with any truly exceptional workplace. But what overall notion enfleshes them and how can they be pursued? Before entering into a fuller discussion, let's pause and examine the notion itself. The idea of 'excellence' has been with us now since at least the time of the Greek philosopher Aristotle, and it deserves some consideration.

EXCELLENCE: A BRIEF ETYMOLOGICAL JOURNEY

The English word "excellence" has as its Latin roots the words *ex* ("out of" or "belonging to") and *celsus* ("the high"). We have the same idea in the familiar Christmas chant of *Gloria in excelsis Deo*, or "Glory to God in the highest." In fact, we often say of someone that they are 'head and shoulders above others': in other words, that a person is "outstanding." Excellence, or going beyond ourselves, is reaching for the heights. But what else is buried in the etymology of this word? By picking up some of these historical clues, we can deepen our insights into its meaning.

The *Oxford English Dictionary* says "excellence" indicates "surpassing merit, virtue." As that definition notes, both merit (*worth*) and virtue are integral to excellence. In fact, both words – "worth" and "virtue" – derive from the Latin *vir* ("man"), a word that also connoted strength (another related word is "virile"). In Anglo-Saxon times, 'worth' was *weorth*, which meant "value." We saw above that excellent companies are *value*-driven; their leaders, like Benedict, are value shapers. Interestingly, the word *weorth* is related to "worship."

This is a critical clue, because it validates our notion that *we do who we are*. Our values tell us what is good, what resonates with our hearts.[1]

Where our hearts are, that is where we put our efforts and priorities. Author James Allen's words are particularly appropriate here: what we most secretly love – whether base or beautiful – is what we will gravitate toward, and by the same token receive "the exact results" of these thoughts – "no more, no less."[2] That is also the focal point for what is implied in the word "worship," which, of course, embraces what Dr. Reuven Bar-On and I describe as spirituality: living life according to what we perceive as ultimately important, meaningful and purposeful. What is true of individuals is true also of organizations. Their excellence – or lack thereof – comes from where their corporate hearts are, how 'valuable' are their coordinating visions, their goals and objectives.

From this journey into ideas, words and word origins, we can draw some rather intriguing conclusions. Pursuing personal excellence involves the desire for virtue or what is truly good, a thirst for identity and uniqueness, and a deep longing for meaning, value and worth. It means setting aside (sacrificing) what will not bring such meaning into our lives in order that the vision or dream of who we are and want to be can be realized. *In Search of Excellence* used the phrase "stick to the knitting," meaning stay on task. Benedict was adamant about consistency and about attending to the details of whatever work one had. To pursue personal excellence, therefore, is to orient our human journey toward the highest possible goals and to remain faithful to – while ever clarifying – our vision and our dream. Since it has deeply personal roots, achieving excellence in the workplace can be done only with respect for the persons involved. Real effort and balance are required to ensure that everyone in the organization becomes deeply committed to the same coordinating vision – not out of any sense of servitude, but as a matter of belief.

In this regard, Benedict pointed out that a leader must go firmly, but balance this attitude with gentleness (RB 64.12, 19). Sir William Honeywood said much the same in Oliver Goldsmith's comedy *The Good-Natured Man* (1768): "We must touch his weaknesses with a delicate hand. There are some faults so nearly allied to excellence, that we can scarce weed out the vice without eradicating the virtue."[3] It is this combination of vision and patience that will make the leader's presence the richest possible and merge the employees' personal commitments to excellence with the company vision. Proceeding with realism but not killing the essence for the sake of the goal, wisdom-leadership maintains a balance, because there will always be the realization that excellence is, in the truest sense of its meaning, a virtue.

EXCELLENCE - A CREATURE OF HABIT

Writer John W. Newbern is credited with saying that there are three kinds of people: those who make things happen, those who watch things happen, and those who wonder what happened.[4] Those who pursue excellence, of course, make things happen. We have been discussing the idea of a coordinating vision that leaders constellate and then facilitate its embrace by organizational members. Centuries before our time, Aristotle recognized the nature of excellence as a virtue; like Newbern, he characterized it as something that stems from habitual practice, that we are what we repeatedly do. In other words, excellence is virtuous behaviour that has become a habit; it is not simply a one-time effort.[5]

Here Aristotle recognized what was essential to the cultivation of excellence. Truly we are creatures of habit. We become *who* we are (the inner) and *what* we do (the outer). The 'doing,' of course, is the result of the thoughts we hold. Key to Benedict's *Rule* is that the monks develop good habits and refuse to indulge in bad ones. With his foundation of a daily *conversatio morum* (a constant reshaping of one's life), Benedict tells his monks that after 'working' the steps required of humility, "good habit and delight in virtue" will come effortlessly (RB 7.69). What seemed impossible or extremely difficult in the beginning will gradually give "inexpressible delight" (P49) – if they stay on task. This principle is by no means confined to monastic life; it is also available to others. The application was broad. Excellence in work was not a result of being given special work to do (7.49). Like Martin Luther King, Benedict considered all work special because of the developed habits of excellence or virtue that could be brought to the task.

EXCELLENCE AND SPIRITUALITY

Since excellence is always the desire for something more, something better, it does not seem at all unnatural that even business writers are beginning to associate the quality of excellence with a spirituality that is drawn to the transcendent. The fact that excellence also involves a certain passion reinforces the same idea. Many of us have heard the expression "a fire in one's belly," referring to being passionate about what matters most to us. Spirituality can be another word for that fire. Excellence is in one sense the 'mad' desire to do the best possible work or to be the best possible person, as if nothing else matters.

Thus, the search for excellence is our ongoing spiritual search, the search for how we can do something more, and do it with fire in our belly. Today especially we are more aware that we live in the age of the spiritual. When Dr. Reuven Bar-On and I normed and validated the Spiritual Quotient Inventory (or SQ-i; see www.sq-i.org) with 1,000 people from 27 countries, 80 percent said they were "spiritual but not religious," a mark of our current times. Positive channelling of this "spiritual" energy can be a mark of excellence, since spirituality by definition is always seeking to go beyond. Over the past 20 years, such an awareness of spirituality has often become part of workplace thinking. In 1995, for example, *Business Week* could write, "Get used to it. Spirituality is creeping into the office… And companies are turning inward in search of a 'soul' as a way to foster creativity and to motivate leaders."[6] *HR Magazine* in 1998 could write, "Yesterday's business motto was 'lean and mean.' Today's business motto is 'lean and meaningful.'"[7] In 2003, Barry Posner, Dean of Business at Santa Clara University, wrote, "Where leaders must go to find their voice is within."[8] Suddenly, a hunger for interiority that became linked with workplace spirituality burst upon the scene: "work is an important component of the spiritual life. … in this sense, all work is a vocation, a calling from a place that is the source of meaning and identity, the roots of which lie beyond human intention and interpretation."[9] Benedict would have said much the same.

The 'turn to the inner' to find the fire in the belly and its desire to pursue excellence is now gaining momentum. Applied to the workplace, a good starting-point definition of workplace spirituality is as follows: "a framework of organizational values evidenced in the culture that promotes employees' experience of transcendence through the work process, facilitating their sense of being connected to others in a way that provides feelings of completeness and joy."[10] When organizations pursue excellence, therefore, employees will experience (1) a meaning-based process in their work, (2) a sense of connectedness to colleagues, and (3) feelings of being engaged, doing an outstanding job with what they are doing. All three, especially the sustenance that comes from the experience of transcendence, will build a culture in which excellence can thrive.

In a similar fashion, Benedict's 'school' was a spiritual vision, which meant in effect that his *Rule* can be understood as a model for daily practice in excellence. Since excellence indicates the quality or qualities of someone who stands out from the rest – is outstanding, exceptional, someone of surpassing merit, or virtue, or *worth* – the *Rule* holds out such an ideal for each individual. If to be engaged means that one has a spiritual agenda, a sense of vocation in one's job, to attain excellence means that the individual now 'works the program,' that is, demonstrates their commitment to excellence in actual deeds. Benedict was capturing Aristotle's notion of excellence as the outcome of habit. But even for Benedict, the *Rule* was simply a training manual, so to speak, a beginner's handbook. Being truly engaged in life and in work was attainable, but only with daily attentiveness and practice, with the goal of excelling at everything one did.

Excellence is the art of doing things well. But it was really only within the context of the community that overall excellence was attained. In addition to its emphasis on balance and moderation, the support and growth of excellence on the spiritual journey and the total commitment to work that it entailed, the *Rule* did not neglect accountability (RB 45-46) and the deep listening that came first (RB 71). The ideal of excellence emerged most fully within the ongoing work of the total community, with the emphasis for excellence in the community's overall well-being. Here, the virtue of "carefulness" (RB 45.2) was essential. In context, the *Rule* is saying that carelessness affects not only the individual, but the whole community as well – that each and every detail involved in both self-responsibility and in being accountable is critical. This involves everyone taking responsibility for themselves and being held accountable by being aware of everyone else in the community. The work and health and engagement of employees in today's organizations, and their quest for excellence, demand no less.

8

BEING PRESENT VS. PRESENTEEISM: ATTENDING TO VS. PUTTING IN TIME

In a time so filled with methods and techniques
designed to change people,
to influence their behavior, and to make them
do new things and think new thoughts,
we have lost the simple but difficult gift of being present
to each other.

—Henri J. M. Nouwen, Donald P. McNeill
and Douglas A. Morrison,
Compassion: Reflections on a Christian Life

Although absenteeism and presenteeism are but two of the symptoms of employee disengagement, they are critical red flags. Even a decade ago, the February 2004 issue of *HR Magazine* pointed out that fully half the world's workforce might be "just going through the motions."[1] While management literature can contain up to nine different definitions of presenteeism, typically it constitutes a mirror image of absenteeism. Whereas absenteeism involves being physically away from the workplace, presenteeism means that one is physically present but mentally or psychologically absent: in other words, just going through the motions. In either instance, the evidence indicates that both the human psyche and organizational effectiveness are suffering angst on a massive basis.

'Being present' was a notion on which Benedict insisted, and which he extended to such concepts as paying attention and staying awake. Before his time, distractions were a major challenge for the desert hermits and for earlier monks, something they had to deal with constantly. Some even went to great lengths – often considered silly by today's standards – to stay on top of things – literally, in the case of St. Simeon the Stylite (c. 390–459) whose claim to fame was that he lived on a small platform on top of a pillar (a stylite) near Aleppo, Syria, for 37 years!

Simeon's solution was extreme. He was certainly present to his divine calling, but to little else. While no less conscious of the crippling effects of the lack of presence, Benedict took a far broader view. In a monastic setting, he certainly wanted his monks to be present to God, but he saw the divine presence all around him, and he expected his monks to be no less present to one another, to their duties and to the wider universe. For him all this was sacred, and he grounded his insistence on presence on self-transcendence. Whether or not a person is religious, such an awareness of presence by becoming 'ex-centric' (moving away from egoism, one's own concerns only) is vital. When we think about it, every act of presence involves some transcendence, for the self is relegated, at least for the moment, to second place, and the other, whether another person, or excellence in what we are doing, or even our presence to the awe of nature becomes more important.

To transpose this to the workplace, the issue is double-sided: being present to what needs to be done, but being present also to our fellow workers. Indeed, Benedict explicitly recognized the importance of presence in terms of work. His own famous statement on work – that "idleness is the enemy of the soul" (RB 48.1) – directly addressed the debilitating effects of absenteeism and presenteeism. One of his *Rule*'s special contributions was to elevate the character of work and endow it with a transcendent quality that gave it meaning, connectedness, purpose and worth. His dictum about idleness recognizes that absence, physical or emotional, and inattentiveness are soul-draining. Benedict sees lack of presence in terms of work as nothing less than as destructive of the person. It would also be destructive of right relationships. Thus, workplace absenteeism and presenteeism, as attitudes of non-caring, take on a deeper meaning. The implication is that workers of every kind need to see their labour as part of their vocation, their calling, capable not only of contributing to their personal growth, but also to the true good of humankind. It is with such an ethical understanding that work's spiritual significance is most fully understood. Seeing work within the notion of calling, a person experiences something of the transcendent. Presence becomes something that will demand a full commitment, but at the same time something that will enrich one's inner life. 'Being there' is static; 'presence' is dynamic.

In that understanding, presence first embraces a responsibility for *interiority*. If we are not present to ourselves, then, given that inner and outer are the same, we can hardly be present to the external world. In the workplace, not only does the organization have a responsibility for fostering and developing a relational context, but employees must do their part as well. The reality testing (RT) competency from Bar-On's Emotional Intelligence-Inventory™ (EQ-i™) and the value of stability (*stabilitas*) that the *Rule* insists upon come into unity here, for employees must learn to be self-responsible and to be anchored (stability) in owning who they are. Lack of presence is not just an organizational problem; it can take a tremendous emotional toll personally. When employees talk about being 'cut off' or 'disconnected' from what they do at work, they are talking about a sense of alienation in the workplace, but also of some deficit in their own sense of self-responsibility inherent in the temptation to presenteeism. Presenteeism – being there in body but absent in mind and spirit – covers those who are emotionally sick of work and who still come to the office each day and simply put in time (to maintain their pension, ride out the string until retirement, etc.). Mark Attridge et al. write that "when health, emotional, worklife, or personal problems interfere with an employee's ability to perform at acceptable levels of productivity, this is considered a presenteeism problem."[2]

But the responsibility, or at least the full responsibility, is not always with the employee. Being present remains always a community concern. It may well be that an employee is not fully disengaged but is coping as best they can within a toxic work environment. In this case, the employee is doing their best in spite of the difficult situation. This could be described as *benign* rather than as *malign* presenteeism. Despite any problems, such employees may simply not want employers to see that they are not committed to their job; this is a situation not so much of disengagement, but of non-engagement. Whatever the situation, what is important is that the worker recognize both the value of workplace presence to oneself and to others, and the personal, relational and organizational costs that the lack of presence can entail.

Indeed, despite any costs of absenteeism and presenteeism to business, the first and most serious costs are to the person. Without experiencing a sense of meaning in work, what often happens is frustration and a disengagement of the employee's person. The philosopher Søren Kierkegaard is noted for saying that many people just live (and work, we assume) their whole life in a state of quiet loneliness. Presenteeism constellates a sense of emptiness inside where nothing supposedly matters, often leading to depression. In this sense, for employees, the depression is a pressing down of emotions that become shadow aspects of the person and a genuine health issue. While the annual financial cost of disabling mental illness is in the hundreds of billions of dollars, the real personal costs are far beyond any reckoning.

Still, just being active – doing things to keep busy – is not necessarily demonstrating presence. On the contrary, the "busy-ness" of today's society is a huge temptation for everyone, and a major source of distraction to personal growth. It can even become a form of presenteeism, much ado about nothing. Benedict acknowledged this when he used the words "above all" (RB 2.33) in cautioning that inordinate attention given to transient or passing affairs of this world is not what it is all about. The challenge of commitment is being open to awareness and learning, the process by which one becomes present in this place rather than someplace else, or an "attitude of place."[3] What is interesting is that in the *Rule*'s opening words, Benedict refers to "drifting"

(P2). This suggests that when we drift, we are inattentive, effectively non-committed. He saw that we drift especially by not listening and not paying attention to one's inner self and to the other. In a real sense, an authentic sense of presence and engagement are synonyms.

In an interesting description of organizational interactions, Iris Vilnai-Yavetz and Anat Rafaeli distinguish between "skeleton" and "tissue" scripts of organizations.[4] The "skeleton" script is the bare bones, the routine business exchanges that take place at work. "Tissue" scripts refer to behaviours above and beyond the minimum that can be "pro social" or "something extra," such as real interpersonal cooperation and empathetic emotions. In practice, presenteeism usually means that to a particular employee, only the "skeleton script" is important. Effectively, the authors are providing a response to presenteeism when they insist that "the tissue script … introduces spirituality into routine organizational interactions."[5] In their view, an approach that takes in employees' "concept of what is best, of what it means to help others be their best, and what it means to feel a sense of connectedness with work and coworkers"[6] – or tissue social behaviours – promotes a sense of both organizational and personal spirituality.[7] On the other hand, since presenteeism means to be present physically at work but absent emotionally and intellectually, such tissue behaviours are usually avoided. But it must be recognized that the result is not just a lack of productivity, but a lack also of interior well-being.

Benedict was practical. He even mentions how one or two senior monks should be assigned to a walk around to make sure the monks were actually working at what they were supposed to be doing (RB 48.17-18). His *Rule* recognized that real idleness or not sticking with the task at hand could become a serious problem. But he was not only being practical; the *Rule* was recognizing the fundamental connection between work and the realm of the spiritual. His monitors were to ensure that any idleness or inattentiveness was minimized so that it did not develop into the larger problem of spiritual disinterest and interior emptiness. In his *Rule*, being engaged, in the sense of being present to any activity, was basic. In fact, one translation[8] speaks of his monks being "engaged" even in the work of reading.

Any discussion of the *Rule*'s contribution to the problem of employee disengagement must be seen within the wider context that the monk is always "in school" (P45). The ordinary worker, as we have noted, must be a constant learner, open to be led on their inward journey in the context of the immediate community and the wider world. The individual is expected to be an active participant on that journey, aligning and attuning oneself to the community's overall mission and to the broader signs of the times that may challenge or modify that context. What the *Rule* not only encourages, but holds essential, is presence in its broadest sense, focusing on one's priorities while not neglecting the bigger picture.

As a responsibility of the whole community, presence involves good leadership. The leader models through inner conviction and example of what is required. In other words, authenticity involves the need to author one's own life and not just to parrot a script. That includes authorship in the workplace. The Celtic spiritual author John O'Donohue (1956–2008) writes that we meet a person's soul or feel that person's presence before we meet that person's body.[9] We experience presence every day at home and at work. Nothing needs to be said, but we realize that who a person is can speak volumes.

This is true of every relationship, but in a work context it is especially important for the relationship that exists between employees and managers. Even when the manager or leader is not personally well known, a perception is created in the mind of the employee that affects their relationship to work. Walking into the hallway can be a positive or negative experience, even before one begins to talk to a colleague, and this is even truer for someone further up in the organizational hierarchy. Indeed, today in larger companies or institutions, while there may be no physical contact, there is connection through such things as email, company blogs, webcasts, TV appearances, large corporate gatherings, and even news of executive salary packages. All of this constitutes leadership presence and creates employee attitudes. We can acknowledge that projection may be evident – that is, one sees what one wants to see – but here is something very tangible: one may even experience a bodily emotion, such as fear, support or indifference.

If we are honest with ourselves, a person's authenticity can be evident to oneself and to others. Such authenticity or lack of authenticity is systemic in the practice and presence of leadership – for good or for ill. There is probably no surer path to disengaged employees than disinterested management. As Benedict recognized, presence is important at every level, but especially on the top floor.

9

BEING TRUE TO SELF AND THE ROLES WE PLAY: DOING WHO WE ARE

To be nobody-but-yourself
– in a world which is doing its best, night and day,
to make you everybody else –
means to fight the hardest battle which any human being can fight;
and never stop fighting.

—e.e. cummings, *A Poet's Advice*, 1958

St. Irenaeus (c. 125–202) has a marvellous saying that has been translated into a popular axiom: "The glory of God is the human being fully alive." We have one purpose in life: to be all that we are called to be. How do we do that? Each of us knows that we often present a false self, one that is not true to who we really are. Jesus was clear about the true self: it is what comes from a person's heart that defiles the person (Mark 7:15). In other words, we 'do' who we are. Above all, Benedict wanted his monks to work daily at becoming more and more who they truly were meant to be. An *inner conviction* of values and truth holds this context firm. Its core is soul first. Management consultant Margaret Wheatley's opening quote to Chapter 4 has set the stage for us: "Leadership is always dependent on the context, but the context is established by the relationships we value."[1] Whatever else happens, the relational establishes this major dynamic in how to be true to our real self and to others. We rise and fall on the basis of the quality and integrity of our relationships. From a leadership perspective, then, I am as successful as a leader as I am as a person.

What psychologist Carl Jung said bears repeating: the inner and the outer are the same. This major clue means that being oneself is not discovered primarily outside a person, by somehow filling an empty space that one experiences when searching and filling it with 'stuff.' Jung's notion of spirituality is one of holy longing for the innate wholeness with which we are born. In today's society, the answer to "And *what* do you do?" often seems to categorize *who* we are. When so much of our identity seems to be shaped by our work, to maintain this inner yearning that is part of our fabric is particularly important because *who* we are – the person – can get lost or eliminated in the *what* we do – our role.

In the workplace, the preservation of personal identity becomes particularly vital on two levels. Obviously, personal identity is essential to the individual so as to preserve their authenticity and realize the fullness of their potential, something that is only recognized over time and experience. But personal identity is equally important to the organizational ethos. Besides all the other responsibilities to grow the company, its leadership needs to honour this yearning for personal growth and meaning that each employee has by nature of being a human being. Such honour and dignity is the touchstone of greatness, of excellence, for everyone and for the organization. Its absence, by either ignoring individual giftedness or trying to force employees into a single mould or role, can be a major obstacle to employee engagement, and can take a particular toll on workplace interrelationships as well as productivity and innovation. The context is strained, if not fractured; role playing becomes the default without much of a personal investment … a recipe for employee disengagement.

We explored the notion of the social character in the Introduction. This social character is prevalent in today's disconnect, that is, in the disengagement of *work* from *worth*. The social character or dominant economic and socio-political structure of society imposes attitudes and behaviours by the socially dominant values without our realizing it. Without reflection, employees, for example, can adopt as 'natural' values that are far from natural in human terms. When managers are steeped in such values and if their style is one of power and control, they end up imposing what they believe and have been taught in MBA school. For example, they may insist that the sole acceptable terms of this social character must emphasize mainly return on investment (ROI) for the shareholders – that is, the fruits of the commodity-based option without its meaning-based ethic. Within this vision of the workplace, commodity-based standards and ideologies are imposed and employees must internalize them in order to fit in.

Unlike in the 19th century and the first half of the 20th century, a major feature of today's workplace is this shift from one of personal achievement to a more impersonal sense. The Abbot at the Benedictine Mount Saviour Monastery in Pine City, New York, says it well:

> My first job was sweeping out the grandstand at the racetrack. My father, in a sense, got me the job, because he knew the man who was the foreman. So, I went to work; I had a responsibility to my father, toward my father's friend and towards the job. It was 35 cents an hour … that's what you were doing; and you felt a certain commitment. Pretty soon people got a job to get something else. You got a job to get money to buy something you wanted. So the job wasn't a job anymore; it was a stepping-stone to something else. And that notion of what I'm doing is a stepping-stone to something else has crept into the culture. So I'm not doing what I'm doing; I've got my eye on something else. And you can't be a monk with your eye on something else.[2]

Employees with their eye on something else cannot work with integrity either. Employees in organizations dominated by a commodity-based vision of the workplace have their eye on something else, such as another opportunity or a transfer to a better job. Work has become solely a productive relationship; one works for someone else with no guarantee of ever seeing the final product. This state of affairs can foster a sense of alienation, disconnection and emotional distress, with the resulting major problem of disengagement that creates a lack of meaning, a lack of control over work processes, powerlessness, working in isolation, a lack of a sense of purpose and involvement in the employee's work, and a lack of social interaction with co-workers.

If the vision and context of the organization is mainly one of shareholder value, this can naturally lead to justifying, for example, cutting a research and development branch because the short-term share price might benefit more from the money saved – plus the executives could receive larger bonuses. There seems to be no long-term concern that shareholders as well as stakeholders might well be seriously damaged by the lack of innovation and the loss of talent to rivals – both of which are major problems and challenges for organizations today. And this does not take into account the social and personal loss created by the laying off of the workforce. In fact, the institutional and corporate world has many terms for justifying commodity-based decisions – terms such as "downsizing," "cutbacks," "voluntary sabbaticals," and "exit incentives," to name a few – all very much in vogue these past three decades.[3]

What I am pointing to here is that we need a revolution of the imagination if we are going to envision a more equitable balance of the commodity-based view with its instrumental purpose of fulfilling needs and preferences *and* the meaning-based view that is not only dedicated to producing and allocating goods and services, but also "insists that the primary characteristic is that it serves as a location where human beings interpret life's meanings."[4] This can be done only if we begin a journey that develops a synergy and honours both being true to our self and being comfortable with the roles we must play at work. It's not an either/or but a both/and commitment.

One critical way that we need to hold firm to our integrity is by examining what we say and do. If, as Jesus says, what comes out of our hearts is the most important concern, then we must take care with our words, because they frame and shape our behaviour. I have repeated the following a number of times: we become that which we love and we become that which we hate. We end up 'doing' who we think we are, personally and corporately. Benedict's *Rule* was well aware of the harm that discourse and words could stir up in a community, because words are not neutral. His chapter on *"Restraint of Speech"* (RB 6) begins with what some might call a shocking statement: that one must be on guard so as not to sin with their tongue (see also Ps. 38[39]: 2-3)! Benedict was also quite strict when the monks had to work at a distance or go out for a short journey (RB 50, 51). We have spoken about his vow of *conversatio morum* – that monks vow to be shaped by the monastic ideals. Thus, going outside on a journey had the potential to be exposed, as we would say today, to the existing social character. Benedict knew that the temptations of the 4 Ps (Persona, Profit, Power and Prestige) embedded in the social character could be very strong enticements. The monks were to be focused and keep to themselves. Mahatma Gandhi's words at the beginning of chapter 1 begin to make even more practical sense: our beliefs do become our thoughts, which in turn are expressed by the words we use and then put into action. Repetitive actions become habits, as we noted with Aristotle, with such habits becoming what we begin to value the most and in turn become and then shape our destiny. Benedict wanted his "school for the Lord's service" (P45) to shape his monks, but saw that "school" as a lifelong and ongoing reflective workshop.

Benedict's stress on the positive value of the daily *conversatio morum* or exposure and openness to the ongoing monastic culture was motivated by his desire that the positive lived values around them could help individuals to shape their lives for the better. At the same time, he did everything to ensure that his community embraced such values. The very heart of Benedict's spirituality on 'obedience' was that the monks vowed stability in order to be obedient and willing to listen to the truth about themselves and not run away from becoming their real selves.[5] But we also know that people are often obliged to live – and work – in situations where the prevailing values are far from positive, life-giving and humane, or where work responsibilities frequently oblige them, or make them oblige themselves, to place themselves in certain roles.

Roles are not necessarily bad. They become costly when we over-identify or place all our energy into the 'role basket.' To come home at the end of a workday and say to one's spouse and children, "Hi, everyone! Dr. So-and-so is here," or "The V.P of Human Resources is back home" comes across as obviously ridiculous and stems from an over-reliance on a commodity-based vision at work. What we find offensive is that the personal dimension is missing; it's the role that walks in the door. Clearly one needs to see oneself in a different and deeper light. It's important to keep in mind that reality becomes a mixture of what is framed and modelled by prevailing social values and how one embodies and lives out these values with people around them. Being locked into a role sends out the signal that 'one is as one does' – an exaggeration if not a distortion of one's inner integrity. 'I am what I do' is one way of expressing this partial truth. While it is probably inevitable that we regularly do this, we should never forget to reflect on the 'who I am' and resist the tendency to shape ourselves, or to allow others to shape us, in inauthentic ways. For Benedict, work was essential and part of one's vocation, but it never exhausted the reality of an individual. We are not just the fruit of our prevailing ethos or the current social character with its contemporary passions and energies. Marketing may try to get us to believe that there is such a reality as "whiter than white" for some products! Being true to self and fluent with the roles we play is its antidote.

In the quote above from the chapter on "Silence" (RB 6.1), Benedict uses the word "sin," a word that most people today may find objectionable. But reflect for a moment on its Greek original: *hamartia* (ἁμαρτάνειν or *hamartánein*), which means "missing the mark." It was only years later that the word "sin" was linked to sexual practices. What is interesting about this etymological connection is that in speaking, many of us do miss the mark. We speak rubbish or perpetuate untruths – this is sometimes called office politics. Thus, we need to ask ourselves on a constant basis about the kinds of thoughts we hold that back up such rubbish. The tragedy of Enron didn't happen overnight. Its sad story is one of certain employees locked into negative roles and personas to the detriment and destruction of the company. A commodity-based vision gone amok where stakeholders had little or no say!

When it comes to employee engagement and workplace satisfaction, the social dimension is immensely important, both in terms of the social milieu that seeks to shape us, too often at the cost of being true to ourselves and instead developing a plastic, surface or false self because of a role we are locked into. But we do have alternatives. Benedict teaches us that upon hearing that a "good life" (P14) is possible, we are to resist other paths, even though this path to being oneself is "narrow" at first. Not only that, but one must "run" (P13) on this path in order to become oneself. But there is great joy in doing so (P49).

A healthy role is something we can enter into but also exit from. In other words, we don't have to be all caught up in role playing; we can be ourselves, not merely a role in which we take part. A study of flight attendants by American sociologist Arlie Russell Hochschild illustrated how employees can disconnect emotionally from the role they are supposed to have while at work.[6] Emotions can be commercialized and performed, especially when an employee must constantly attend to passengers' wishes and always show a pleasant face. But a flight attendant who never puts aside the role has a problem. We would ask, "Who is the person beneath the role?" We ask this question because we know there is something more to the person: a depth, an interiority. Hochschild referred to this workplace role-playing as deep acting: for some flight attendants she describes, that meant creating the illusion, at least, of good service irrespective of interior feelings.

Clearly, the constant workplace role-playing that would involve the suppression of one's feelings can lead to employee disengagement. It involves an absence of connections and energy and a defensive withdrawal of the person's self, so that a worker becomes in a sense automatic or robotic – in other words, the person enters into what we can call 'playing a role' and is never themselves to any great extent. Professor William Kahn, an authority on employee engagement, sees disengagement resulting from the loss of three key psychological conditions: (1) *meaningfulness*, defined as "the feeling that one is receiving a return on investments in a currency of physical, cognitive or emotional energy. People experienced such meaningfulness when they felt worthwhile, useful and valuable – as though they made a difference and were not taken for granted"; (2) *safety*, explained as "feeling able to show and employ one's self without fear of negative consequences to self-image, status, or career … When situations were unclear, inconsistent, unpredictable, or threatening, personal engagement was deemed too risky or unsafe"; and (3) *availability* or "the sense of having the physical, emotional, or psychological resources to personally engage at a particular moment. It measures how ready people are to engage, given the distractions they experience as members of social systems."[7]

What underscores these conditions are the varying degrees of self that a person feels they can apply physically, cognitively and emotionally in the workplace. Recent surveys on workplace engagement have come to see disengagement primarily as an emotional disconnect. In this "uncoupling," as Kahn calls it, "of selves from work roles, in disengagement, people withdraw and defend themselves physically, cognitively, or emotionally during role performances."[8] Put another way, engagement is the extent to which employees go the extra mile and put their true selves into their work – contributing more of their energy, creativity and passion on the job. Benedict would have wholeheartedly given his approval (RB 48.8).

People find themselves in many job roles over time or even at the same time. Within the workplace, roles need to take into account and allow for flexibility in life and workplace balance, the meaningfulness of the job, whether the organization is committed to corporate social responsibility, interpersonal relationships, variety in work, and the work itself. While the individual's self-conception and reflection are essential, much also depends on the workplace culture. As in Benedict's monastery, a healthy positive environment can be absorbed to personal benefit; negative attitudes and expectations can do individual damage. Research has found that managers' emotional intelligence significantly correlates with the job satisfaction of the employees they manage. My colleague, Dr. Reuven Bar-On, wrote to me about the levels of interaction in this relationship between the organization and the individual's self-image, and the connection to emotional intelligence (EI):

In light of the fact that senior managers often set the tone for the people they manage and the atmosphere at work, this indicates that their EI explains part of the dissatisfaction in the workplace. And in light of the fact that their EI explains more about organizational effectiveness/productivity than it does about the feeling of employee satisfaction at work, this possibly means that there must be something else that explains why employees feel dissatisfied and possibly disengaged. And this could be because of a feeling of disconnect between their set of values and a sense of purpose and what their place of employment provides in this regard.[9]

What Bar-On is pointing to is the 'something more' – the reality of meaningfulness – or the spiritual dimension called *meaning* that is not addressed by the organization. Organizations have spent enormous amounts of time and money on employee satisfaction surveys, but have not truly addressed the need that employees have for a meaning-based workplace as they have for a commodity-based workplace. Both are necessary to develop a *worth*place – honouring each person's dignity and getting the work done.

Personal resilience allows us to enter and exit work roles. Reality requires that we assume certain work roles; reality also requires that we be ourselves. Hence, the Benedictine emphasis on balance once more applies: "The Benedictine does not so much follow an horarium, or rigid daily schedule, as arrange a balance of life activities. The Benedictine does not so much follow a set of behaviors as develop an *attitude of place* in the universe that guides every conversation and every common act."[10] A person's adaptability and fluency is in knowing how to shift when required. The workaholic does not ever leave the work role. When someone says, "They don't have a personal life," sadly, this is often more true than not. Awareness of one's shadow motivations and their energies (e.g., the temptations of the 4 Ps – Persona, Profit, Power and Prestige), and the yearning for soul is the basis for effective discernment. That alone provides balance. Roles people enjoy, for instance, are then embraced; roles they do not like are disregarded. In work environments, a similar calibration of self-in-role occurs, leading to the individual's engagement or disengagement. In a workplace role, one can either bring in one's personal self or leave it out. That people self-express is normal. Of course, there is always the danger that with an imbalance, a workplace role can take over.

It is obvious how crucial is our personal connectedness to depth, our fidelity to our inner soul, for being oneself. When we stop and reflect, we realize that the tapestry that is our life does in fact hang together. There is a connecting of the dots. Soul, our inner centre, is always at work shaping us and making whole what we too often see only as single threads in the tapestry of our lives. While we can get lost along the way and lose our balance, if we listen to the soul's call often enough and long enough, as Benedict asks us, we will become ourselves and still engage in the roles we must play. In the words of the Trappist monk Thomas Merton,

> Life consists in learning to live on one's own, spontaneous, freewheeling: to do this one must recognize what is one's own – be familiar and at home with oneself. This means basically learning who one is, and learning what one has to offer the contemporary world, and then learning how to make that offering valid.[11]

10

THE BIG PICTURE: EMPLOYEE ENGAGEMENT AND COMPANY EXCELLENCE

In monastic spirituality, then,
leadership is not intent on making things right;
leadership is intent on making life right.

—Joan Chittister, *The Rule of Benedict: Insights for the Ages*, 1992

"Making life right." For real people. In real workplace situations. Such has been our theme throughout this book. No one would pretend that this is an easy task; it takes real effort on the part of both organizations and employees. But it is not an impossible task. The principles for new insights into working life and workplace situations are there. Some of them come from good business practices. Some are found in the better understanding and application of emotional intelligence. And some, as will have been evident from previous chapters, come from viewing the workplace in a spiritual context – that term being understood in its very broadest sense.

Still, what must come first is the recognition of disengagement. Although the reality is widespread, serious discussion of it has been lacking. Even in early January 2014, Gallup was describing only five strategies to build what it called the organization's "constituency of engaged employees": (1) using "the right employee engagement survey," (2) focusing "on engagement at the local and organizational levels," (3) selecting "the right managers," (4) coaching managers and holding them "accountable for their employees' engagement," and (5) defining "engagement goals in realistic, everyday terms." With so much supporting research evidence over the past 25 years, Gallup makes no mention of acknowledging the issue of workplace spirituality as a valid sixth way![1] For their part, organizations might be prone to see disengagement as an admission of corporate failing – "Not in our company, certainly!" The employees who are affected by it may tend to think that it is an individual phenomenon, something that affects only them, or they may recognize the symptoms but not the underlying reality – a spiritual *dis*-ease, as Benedict would have proclaimed. Even the enormous presence of depression in the workplace is not acknowledged. While the Canadian economy, according to a 2004 World Health Organization study, was losing up to $51 billion annually due to mental health and addiction issues, almost $20 billion of those costs involved workplace losses.[2] One newspaper even referred to Ottawa, Canada's capital city, and its thousands of federal employees as the "depression capital of Canada"! Bill Wilkerson, co-founder of the Global Business and Economic Roundtable on Addiction and Mental Health, candidly says, "The federal workplace, make no mistake about it, makes people sick. It's a distressed and dismayed workplace."[3] There can be no fix without acknowledging that something needs fixing, and there cannot be a proper fix without understanding a problem fully.

It is clear from even a superficial reading of the *Rule of Benedict* that while the intellectual dimension is never lacking, its total context relies equally upon emotional and spiritual wisdom. The question that needs addressing is the following: "What in particular does the spirituality of Benedict contribute to workplace spirituality that will shine a light on the 'something more' that the application of emotional intelligence theory alone cannot offer?" While the *Rule* is eclectic – having its own innate character that cannot easily be systematized – its spiritual core has nevertheless been an inspiration for fifteen centuries. Moreover, while it is clearly a Christian document, its application to the workplace can embrace the understanding that Kees Waaijman, a Dutch Carmelite and professor of spirituality, describes: "In our daily life, as a rule, spirituality is latently present as a quiet force in the background, an inspiration and an orientation."[4] For Benedict, this meant that everything that existed had a transcendent character, that the presence of God was literally everywhere: in things, places and people. Even garden tools must be seen and handled as "sacred vessels" (RB 31.10). Brian Draper, former editor of the U.K.'s *Third Way* magazine, likens spirituality as bridging who we are and what we do,[5] the connecting link between being and action, between our values and our ethics, what we described in an earlier section as truly 'doing who we are.'

This 'something more,' the spirituality to be derived from Benedict's fundamental principles, is the importance of transcendence in everyday life and the acknowledgement of reality beyond one's self, the recognition of community and the connectedness of self to all other things, and a purposeful care in attending to the ordinary events of each day while maintaining a sense of balance in what one does. All of these can help us understand more profoundly the contemporary workplace experience.

The innate reality and experience of transcendence is central. The word 'climb' is etymologically related to the word 'transcendence,' most directly from the Latin *transcendere* or "climb over or beyond, surmount, overstep." The American poet John Gillespie Magee, Jr. (1922–1941), a Royal Canadian Air Force Spitfire pilot during World War II, reminds us that even in the midst of life itself we can climb the heights. His poem "High Flight" reflects his own experience of transcendence, that there is always something more, something beyond:

Oh! I have slipped the surly bonds of earth …
And, while with silent lifting mind I've trod
The high untrespassed sanctity of space,
Put out my hand and touched the face of God.[6]

Recognizing transcendence is not only an individual need. The organization's mission becomes possible when it creates the conditions through which employees are engaged and the workplace encourages them to look to 'something beyond.' Work is not only objective (its content) but also subjective (its meaning). Appreciating this prevents employees from simply viewing themselves as cogs in the company machine. But for that to happen, transcendence must be embraced and embedded in the overall organizational vision. As has been suggested, true engagement can result only when this vision rests not only on the *technical* competencies required (commodity-based products, services, etc.), not only on the *emotional* fluency of employees (emotional intelligence awareness), but also on work's *inherent transcendent dynamism* (meaning-based connectedness).

What is essential to the notion of transcendence in Benedict's *Rule* is that it is never removed from the commitment to the ordinariness of life that is found in its every precept. From a Benedictine perspective, this allows us to realize that everything in life is filled with the potential for wholeness. That wonderful insight of Teresa of Avila (1515–1582) says it well: "God is found among the pots and pans!" Benedict was a realist. Humility, as in being down to earth or accepting reality as it occurs, is necessary to breathe such spirituality, to prevent false confidence by trying to avoid acknowledging reality. Benedict's understanding of humility is for people to be themselves, to be honest about who they really are, as raw as that can be at times. It is an acceptance that wholeness lies in the ordinariness of living, that appreciating the daily reality around us leads to understanding and accepting our personal limitations.

It's obvious how spirit, then, is intimately connected with being engaged in life, in work and in the building of the *worth*place. It's probably strange for some business people to read about transcendence and relate it to doing business. But Henry Margenau, the physicist and philosopher of science, said that the only difference between ourselves and the mystic is that "the mystic is able to peek through the keyhole of reality and see the truth."[7] When transcendence is rooted in reality, our personal lives are animated spiritually in all that we do; so are our work lives. Properly understood, Benedict's spirituality then becomes an intrinsic animating force, an energy that propels us into living every aspect of life to the fullest.

In a similar manner, Benedict's spirituality never excluded the conscious development of the human qualities needed to make interior dispositions truly purposeful. Indeed, he saw the development of the human and emotional dimensions of the person as foundational for personal transcendence. Within this context, work was a vital humanizing factor. Indeed, one author, as we have seen, rephrases Benedict's great aphorism on work as follows: that work is "the friend of the soul."[8] Within work itself there is something life-giving and necessary to living life well. Benedict saw work as building a sense of personal worth; at the same time, it contributed to the wider world. Joan Chittister put it this way: "Work is not to enable me to get ahead; the purpose of work is to enable me to get more human and to make my world more just."[9] This single sentence expresses the humanism, the respect for the individual and the social responsibility that are intrinsic to Benedict's concept of work.

In this sense, humanness and transcendence are blended into a Benedictine notion of connectedness that can revitalize the workplace. Work is not for the individual's sake alone; in its fullest measure it is an act of charity. In its narrowest sense, connectedness embraces the immediate community. Work was a common enterprise needed to sustain the economic and social needs of the community and its individual members. But even here there was a deeper sense of connectedness, for work also involved a deep respect for fellow workers, their individual talents, and even their shortcomings (RB 72.5). It was a venture undertaken *together*. But Benedict's notion of the value and nature of work stretched beyond the confines of the local community. There was also a deep sense of social responsibility. Monks worked to be economically independent and not to be a burden to others in society (RB 48.8). Not only that – being self-sufficient allowed them to attend to the needs of the less fortunate. Producing more than they needed for themselves made possible the charitable acts of welcoming guests and strangers and giving alms to those in need. For Benedict, connectedness went even beyond the personal. There was a sense of ecology here, a sense of using created things in the wisest possible way. In other words, the Benedictine vision acknowledges that the earth and its peoples are not here to care for us; we are here to care for them. Work develops both us and the world around us – in justice and for the greatest good.

It is impossible to read the *Rule of Benedict* without recognizing that on every page, recognition of a higher purpose demanded a commitment to excellence in all things, the workplace included. One scholar notes that Benedict insisted "on performing work with a particular care," a disposition inspired by "a sense of respect."[10] The diligent individual puts in the effort to do a good job, respecting people, places and things, and thus exercises an ethic of care, working *care-fully* in that word's broadest sense. This sense of doing work and doing it well is a commitment of the whole person; it has value in and of itself and it gives meaning to the worker. Still, Benedict's notion of excellence was never individualistic. While based in and for the growth of the individual, it had to be envisioned and lived in relation to a community of other persons. It enabled learning from one another. It also enabled the generation of new ideas and approaches, being able to think outside the box. And in the end, excellence served both the community itself and the community's wider mission.

The recognition of the scope and nature of employee disengagement has brought us to see how a combined emotional and spiritual response might minimize its effects and address even some of its root causes. The reference is to a response, not to responses, for although emotional intelligence and spirituality deal with different orders, there is a clear interconnection between them. To turn to only one of these and to ignore possible contributions from the other would be a real oversight. Taking them together can provide broader insights and a more effective overall approach in addressing the real problems.

Our focus has been on the *Rule of Benedict*, which has to be credited with providing both a profound awareness of human nature and a deeply interiorized, but eminently practical and practised, spirituality. Obviously, as an ancient monastic rule, it cannot be immediately used to transform the modern secular workplace. Put bluntly, the monastic vocation is not for everybody, and a monastic spirituality will have its differences – such as vowed celibacy – that will have to be addressed otherwise. At the same time, Benedict's *Rule* contains a wisdom that, when distilled, is no less profitable for today's world. It contains a richness of emotional and spiritual content that can be transposed beyond the monastery walls and be applied to the human situation generally and to organizational theory and to the workplace particularly.

Above all, Benedict brought 'worth' to 'work.' Work was a value, not just an obligation or a necessity. Indeed, Benedict exalted work, seeing in it a transcendent character. Today's workers have experienced increasingly that something is missing in the workplace. While acknowledging that making a profit and earning a salary – work's objective dimensions – are important, those in the workplace are now also beginning to realize that work without a sense of personal meaning and purpose – the subjective good – is not acceptable. Benedict's understanding of work as conveying worth leads him to start with the subjective, with the person as foundational. Work is the expression of the person; the person's work reverberates back to defining and shaping who the person becomes. The great need today is the task of taking business and organizations out of a one-dimensional approach so they can have a wider vision. Thankfully, such thinking is now beginning to emerge. One business professor put it like this: "We should be thinking of the corporation as a voluntary and evolving community that can either help or prevent people from realizing their essential humanity."[11] Indeed, the widespread presence of workplace disengagement means that similar thinking might not only be beneficial to the individual employee and the company community, but bring tangible benefits even in business terms.

In his own way, Benedict recognized the need for both. For the individual, he wanted work to be meaningful in every sense. At the same time, he wanted the work of his monasteries to be profitable. The difference was in how he would use the profits – for alms and guests, to support monks who were infirm, to keep up the monastery fabric. Meaning and profit might seem like strange bedfellows. In some contemporary quarters, the thought of blending the two may never have occurred; in others, there might be a nagging sense of conflict. Still, to any who might say that the subjective and objective dimensions of work are inherently incompatible, two things need to be said. First, it must be observed that spirituality of itself is transformational; it can make a difference in everything from excellence to innovation. Then, too, to anyone familiar with either cheeses or liqueurs, the Benedictine tradition itself stands as a concrete retort.

At the organizational level, Benedict offered solid principles that can easily be applied to today's workplace – flexibility, moderation, empathy, social responsibility and single-mindedness. But behind them is his vision that work should have meaning for the individual, build up the community and contribute to the higher good. While his counsels are always practical, since they account for human nature, it is ultimately this broader, transcendent vision of Benedict that can facilitate the shift from *work*place to *worth*place.

REFLECTIONS
ON OUR WORK LIFE

Benedict's Chapter 4, "Tools of Good Works," contains practical learning steps, what we can call his 'curriculum.' Benedict's own words can be our tools for thinking about our working life. In this short section, sayings from his *Rule* are followed by a short question for further reflection. The key idea is in *italics*.

- Benedict writes, "Are you looking for a better life" (P15) or are you simply wishy-washy, "with a character as soft as lead"? (RB 1.6). In other words, are you a *seeker*, willing to do what it takes to be all you can be?

- Benedict writes [of a type of monk], "Always on the move, they never settle down" (RB 1.11). In other words, does being truly rooted [*stabilitas*] as a person matter to you and to your work?

- Benedict writes, "Anyone who receives the name of abbot is to lead his disciples by … point[ing] out to them all that is good and holy more by example than by words" (RB 2.11-12). In other words, is *authority* for you relational, or more a matter of power and control; are you prepared to 'walk the talk' in what you say and do?

- Benedict writes, "The abbot is to show equal love to everyone and apply the same discipline to all according to their merits" (RB 2.22). In other words, do you practise *equity and fairness* in your day-to-day workplace situations?

- Benedict writes, "The basic road to progress for the humble person is through prompt obedience" (RB 5.1). In other words, can you embrace the value of *deep listening* and being honest with yourself to keep your finger on the important things around you?

- Benedict writes, "A disciple who obeys grudgingly and grumbles, not only aloud but also in his heart, ... even though they carry out the order, ... they will have no reward" (RB 5.17, 19). In other words, do you have a habit of *grumbling*, even under your breath, of digging in your heels, or can you do your work with a sense of openness?

- Benedict writes, "... there are times when good words are to be left unsaid out of esteem for silence" (RB 6.2). In other words, do you think before you speak, and will what you are going to say improve on the *silence*?

- Benedict writes, "We have already established the order for ...Vigils and Lauds. Now let us arrange the remaining hours" (RB 17.1). In other words, can you appreciate how *order* in daily living can bring a sense of serenity and balance to the ordinariness of everyday tasks and responsibilities?

- Benedict writes, "They are to be chosen for virtuous living and wise teaching, not for their rank" (RB 21.1) In other words, if you have people for whom you are responsible, can you develop them as *people of character*, not just because they are useful?

- Benedict writes, "He will regard all utensils and goods ... as sacred vessels of the altar, aware that nothing is to be neglected" (RB 31.10-11). In other words, are you *care-ful* with the resources you use, and, above all, *care-ful* in how you relate with your colleagues?

- Benedict writes, "... the old and the young ... should be treated with kindly consideration" (RB 37.1, 3). In other words, would your fellow workers say you are a person who acts with that kind of *compassion* in the face of others' needs?

- Benedict writes, "On hearing the signal ... the monk will immediately set aside what he has in hand ..." (RB 43.1). In other words, are you *tardy* or do you respect the time of the other people you work with?

- Benedict writes, "If someone commits a fault while at work ... he must at once come before the abbot and community and of his own accord admit his fault" (RB 46.1, 3). In other words, do you accept being *accountable* for what happens in your personal and working life?

- Benedict writes, "When they live by the labor of their hands … then they are really monks" (RB 48.8). In other words, can you envision your work as a vocation, as something *sacred*, or is work simply a T.G.I.F. affair?

- Benedict writes, "Proper respect should be shown to *all*" (RB 53.2). In other words, are you gracious with your *hospitality* in the workplace, open to receiving others, noticing who they are, paying attention to them, being present to them, making a 'safe space' for them?

- Benedict writes, "Monks must not complain about the color or texture of [their clothing], but use what is available in the vicinity at a reasonable cost" (RB 55.7). In other words, can you *just be you* without putting on airs, wielding power, flaunting your income, and saying in so many words how important you are?

- Benedict writes, "The one to be received, however, must first promise his stability, fidelity to the monastic lifestyle [*conversatio morum*] and obedience before all in the oratory" (RB 58.17). In other words, can you be faithful to the *committed relationship* your job entails and at the same time its ongoing demands for *personal change*?

- Benedict writes, "If, after his suggestion, the superior does not change his mind or his order, the junior monk should realize it is in his best interest" (RB 68.4). In other words, can you allow yourself to be open to the new, the strange, the seemingly impossible, to what you think is *beyond* your capabilities?

STUDY GUIDE

Prepared by

Michael Rock
(M.Th., L.Th., Ed.D.)

with discussion questions to help facilitate
small-group discussions,
parish retreats and
workshop presentations

<u>Word from the author</u>: You might find it very helpful to have a small note-book to jot down ideas that are meaningful to you or that strike you as help-ful from your discussions. Date the entries. This notebook becomes your Journal; you can always refer back to it. Doing this is also a key to developing an inner sense of your life – a factor that is a theme throughout the book.

PREFACE

<u>Theme</u>: a description of the ongoing challenge that has been with us since the beginning of humankind: that the "barbarian," that is, the undeveloped side of ourselves, is still alive and well in each of us. Socrates' counsel is still required today: "Know thyself." That is, learn to confront and acknowledge this 'inner barbarian' or shadow side or "Primitive Person" (Dr. Carl Jung).

Questions to consider:

- What "barbarians" do you think "have already been governing us for quite some time"?

- What does the expression "we become that which we love, but we also become that which we hate" mean to you?

- What would your 'inner barbarian' look like and feel like?
- *"All change begins from the inside out."* What do you make of that statement?
- How does "we *do* who we are" apply to you personally and in your workplace?

Reflective quote: "Inside each of us is a little tyrant who wants power and the associated prestige, who wants to dominate, to be superior and to control. We feel we are the only ones to seek the truth – and that, sometimes, in the name of God. There is nothing more terrible than a tyrant using religion as his or her cover." – Jean Vanier, *Community and Growth*, p. 216.

INTRODUCTION

Theme #1 ("Today's Disengagement Crisis"): the enormous problem of workplace disengagement that, at its heart, is an emotional problem, including a short discussion on emotional intelligence (EQ) as it invites a natural linkage and *bridging* to the sixth-century *Rule of Benedict* in shaping EQ into a life-giving context.

Questions to consider:

- What is today's workplace disengagement crisis all about?
- "The business paradigm needs a major overhaul." Discuss.
- What are some of the symptoms of workplace disengagement?
- Dr. Daniel Goleman says there is "a new yardstick" and "a different way of being smart." What is he implying?
- How does emotional intelligence act as a 'stepping stone' and "a glimpse into the transcendence of the human person"?

Reflection: "The vast majority of employed people around the globe are 'not engaged' or 'actively disengaged' at work, meaning they are emotionally disconnected from their workplaces and less likely to be productive." – Gallup Global Workplace Report (2013)

* * * * * * *

<u>Theme #2</u> ("Re-Valuing Work: the *Rule of Benedict*): an understanding of the *person* doing the work by integrating St. Benedict's basic monastic principles and values, his leadership attributes, and his approach to a spirituality of work.

Questions to consider:

- "A missing ingredient when it comes to employee disengagement is acknowledging the person doing the work." Discuss.

- What did John Paul II mean when he said there are objective as well as subjective dimensions of work?

- St. Benedict wanted "to establish a school" for his monastic purposes. How would today's concept of the *learning organization* support his goal?

- How could Benedict's basic values of *stability* (*stabilitas*), *conversion of life* (*conversatio morum*), and *obedience* (*obœdientia*, as deep listening) contribute to well-being in today's workplaces?

- In Benedict's language, *idleness* was "the enemy of the soul" (RB 48). What did he mean by that and how can his intuition be helpful for us today?

Reflection: "Spiritual intelligence represents our drive for meaning and connection with the infinite." – Stephen Covey

SECTION I: THE CORE VISION

CHAPTER 1: Work as a Calling: Maturity and Stability

<u>Theme</u>: a discussion of the contemporary reality and problem of workplace instability and restlessness, a problem exacerbated by a culture of instant gratification, modern technology, employees not often seeing their work as a *calling* or part of their real selves, and the ever-present seductions (4Ps) that contribute to this ongoing rootedness.

Questions to consider:

- If stability or rootedness (*stabilitas*) is so important, how can the ideas of "multitasking" or promoting "employee flexibility" make any sense?

- How does 'putting your life *in order*' help you to live more spiritually?
- How does one become "ex-centric" in developing a deeper and a "larger consciousness" or "rootedness"?
- As described in the chapter, how do the distractions or idols or seductions of the mind around the 4Ps (*Persona, Profit, Power* and *Prestige*) affect you personally?

Reflection: "They who reach down into the depths of life where, in the stillness, the voice of God is heard, have the stabilizing power which carries them poised and serene through the hurricane of difficulties." – Spencer W. Kimball

CHAPTER 2: Working Together: Work and Community

Theme: a discussion on how connectedness and belonging are the world's driving forces. Community is "a context 'ideal' for personal growth, both emotional and spiritual."

Questions to consider:
- Why do you have or not have a "home" page on the Internet?
- Why would Benedict describe community as one that constantly anticipates "what is better for someone else"?
- How do you explain Benedict's idea of "competitive experience" as one whereby "its members should try to outdo one another in respecting others?
- How would you explain the following four challenging coordinates that Benedict demands for community: respect, patience, openness, action?
- Why is community an 'ideal' context for personal life, both emotional and spiritual?

Reflection: "The smallest indivisible human unit is two people, not one; one is a fiction. From such nets of souls societies, the social world, human life springs." – Tony Kushner

CHAPTER 3: The Golden Rule for the Workplace:
The Dignity of Our Colleagues

<u>Theme</u>: a discussion on Chapter 7, "Humility," of the *Rule of Benedict*, as 'translated' into meaningful notions for the contemporary person.

Questions to consider:

- Why does Marcus Buckingham say in the opening quote, "The best managers break the Golden Rule every day"?
- What does the Golden Rule mean to you?
- After you read the 12 "Tips," what is the one Tip that you find the most challenging to accomplish in your day-to-day living?
- Why would Benedict have as his first step (or, TIP #1) that we should make sure our priorities are straight?
- How does Benedict's 12 steps of humility (or, Tips #1–12) embrace the ethic of the Golden Rule to "create for us a path, a path for life itself and for our work life"?

Reflection: "Everything that is in the heavens, on the earth, and under the earth is penetrated with connectedness, penetrated with relatedness." – Hildegard of Bingen

* * * * * * *

SECTION II: PRACTICE AT WORK

CHAPTER 4: Enlightened Leadership and Decision Making

<u>Theme</u>: a discussion on the most important – and countercultural – description of the purpose of leadership: "of creating context" by establishing life-affirming relationships.

Questions to consider:

- How can you expand on Dr. Margaret Wheatley's comment: "Leadership is always dependent on the context, but the context is established by the relationships we value"?
- Why is wisdom so critical "in the thinking and feeling needed for leadership"?

- What qualities did some of the wisdom-leaders you have known possess?
- How has the "fear of foolishness" affected you, personally or in the workplace?
- In what ways do the "red flags" that can impact making decisions influence you in your decision-making efforts?

Reflection: "... the fear of foolishness is essential to wisdom. Unfortunately, leaders are often conditioned to suppress fear in favor of confidence. ... wise leaders fear foolishness while foolish leaders are fearless. Leaders fall into traps and hit walls that result in fallacies. It is the recognition of these fallacies and the fear of their consequences that compel leaders to seek wisdom." – Prof. Stephanie T. Solansky

CHAPTER 5: The Art of Listening: The New Obedience

Theme: a discussion on the importance of the art of listening that includes both a cognitive element of *understanding* and an affective element of *accepting* others as well as attending to the other – an "ex-centric" activity – and listening with the ear of one's heart.

Questions to consider:

- What are some examples of your own efforts to listen well?
- How do you find stillness in a world that has so much noise?
- How challenging is it to *notice* and *attend to* what is happening during each day?
- How would attending to an "ecology of emotions" make a difference in your life?
- How would you explain to someone the concept of "listening as the new obedience"?

Reflection: "There's a lot of difference between listening and hearing." – G.K. Chesterton

* * * * * * *

SECTION III: RESPONDING TO SYMPTOMS OF DISENGAGEMENT

CHAPTER 6: Openness to Creativity: The Spirit of Curiosity

<u>Theme</u>: a discussion on openness to the creativity in personal and workplace contexts, and to realizing that being 'learned' intellectually is no guarantee to this openness, since it demands passion and openness to real feelings to counteract declining innovation.

Questions to consider:

- What challenges does Benedict's concept of *coversatio morum* or 'openness to change' offer to you?
- What do the words "a sense of the transcendent will always look for 'something more'" mean for you?
- How can you more fully embrace Aristotle's idea of "the power of curiosity"?
- If the fibre for the context of leadership is a relational one, what challenges do leaders and managers have toward their employees?
- What do you imagine is the connection between Benedict's notion of 'a listening heart' and openness to creativity?

Reflection: "It is, in fact, nothing short of a miracle that the modern methods of instruction have not entirely strangled the holy curiosity of inquiry." – Albert Einstein

CHAPTER 7: The Pursuit of Excellence: Building Worth

<u>Theme</u>: a discussion of excellence in the 'ordinariness' of daily life, noting that spirituality, at its base, is living life according to what one perceives as ultimately important, meaningful and purposeful, and the fruit of our habitual practices.

Questions to consider:

- What is implied in the opening quote by Martin Luther King?
- How are 'beliefs,' as understood by IBM's founder, Thomas Watson, Jr., linked to the idea of "excellence"?

- Using a scale of 1 to 10, what would be your rating of your workplace for each of the seven beliefs summarized from *In Search of Excellence*?

- How is the idea from the etymology of 'excellence' helpful to explain the notion that *we do who we are*?

- In what way is your understanding of 'spirituality' descriptive of the way you live?

Reflection: "My meaning simply is, that whatever I have tried to do in life, I have tried with all my heart to do well; that whatever I have devoted myself to, I have devoted myself to completely; that in great aims and in small, I have always been thoroughly in earnest." – Charles Dickens, *David Copperfield*

CHAPTER 8: Being Present vs. Presenteeism: Attending to vs. Putting in Time

Theme: a discussion on how 'being present' necessarily involves, to some extent, an experience of transcendence, a sense of presence by which Benedict elevated the character of work.

Questions to consider:

- When do you find yourself simply tuning out co-workers or family members?

- How does one experience 'transcendence' in a work situation?

- How can you link the notion of 'presence' with that of 'interiority'?

- What is your experience of 'presenteeism' in the workplace?

- What would be your explanation of John O'Donohue's idea that "we meet a person's soul or feel that person's *presence* before we meet that person's body"?

Reflection: "Your true home is in the here and the now." – Thích Nhất Hạnh

CHAPTER 9: Being True to Self and the Roles We Play: Doing Who We Are

Theme: a discussion on fleshing out St. Irenaeus' statement that the glory of God is the human being fully alive and Carl Jung's notion that spirituality is one of holy longing to help us know the difference between *who* we are (the person) and *what* we do (the role).

Questions to consider:

- How do you honour the yearning for personal growth and meaning in your work situation?
- What does it mean to say that today's "social character" contains a compelling element of "disconnect"?
- In your workplace, how does it come across when employees keep their "eye on something else" a lot of the time?
- What kinds of roles are in your "role basket"?
- How would you connect Benedict's notion of "restraint of speech" (RB 6), office politics, and being true to oneself?

Reflection: "If you don't watch it people will force you one way or the other, into doing what they think you should do, or into just being mule-stubborn and doing the opposite out of spite." – Ken Kesey, *One Flew Over the Cuckoo's Nest*

CHAPTER 10: The Big Picture: Employee Engagement and Company Excellence

Theme: a discussion on summarizing the key points in developing employee engagement and organizational excellence in the building of the *worth*place and how the spirituality of Benedict brought 'worth' to 'work' so that *meaning* and *profit* can be companions.

Questions to consider:

- How does one make life "right," for real people and in real workplace situations?
- What is a full answer to the problem of employee disengagement?

- What is meant when the U.K.'s *Third Way* editor likens spirituality to bridging *who* we are and *what* we do?
- How can work become a vital humanizing factor?
- How would you explain the idea of working *care-fully*?

Reflection: "You manage things; you lead people." – Rear Admiral Grace Hopper

NOTES

DEDICATION

1   Demetrius Dumm, O.S.B., *Cherish Christ Above All: The Bible in the Rule of Benedict* (New York: Paulist Press, 1996), 99.

PREFACE

1   Alisdair MacIntyre, *After Virtue: A Study in Moral Theory* (London: Duckworth, 1981), 275.

INTRODUCTION

1   "Worldwide, Only 13% of Employees Are Engaged at Work" (Gallup Inc., *State of the Global Workplace Report*, 2013), 11–13.

2   A description by my colleague Dr. Reuven Bar-On (author of the world-famous Emotional Quotient-*Inventory*™, or EQ-i™), and me in the design, norming and validation of the Spiritual Quotient Inventory™ (or SQ-i™) and its applications. See www.sq-i.org.

3   Nigel Marsh, "How to Make Work-life Balance Work," TED Talk, filmed May 2010. http://www.ted.com/talks/nigel_marsh_how_to_make_work_life_balance_work. Located at 1:28 of the 10:05 min. talk: "... they [people] work long, hard hours at jobs they hate to enable them to buy things they don't need to impress people they don't like."

4   T.S. Eliot, "The Hollow Men," I.

5   Peter J. Frost, *Toxic Emotions at Work and What You Can Do About Them* (Cambridge, MA: Harvard Business Press, 2007), 35.

6   Charles Darwin, *The Expression of the Emotions in Man and Animals* (Chicago: University of Chicago Press, 1872/1965).

7   David Wechsler, "Nonintellective Factors in General Intelligence," *The Journal of Abnormal and Social Psychology*, Vol. 38, no. 1 (January 1943): 101–103.

8   Daniel Goleman, *Working with Emotional Intelligence* (New York: Bantam Books, 1998), 3, 4.

9   Studies cited by Michael Cox and Michael E. Rock, *The 7 Pillars of Visionary Leadership: Aligning Your Organization for Enduring Success* (Toronto: Harcourt Brace & Company, 1997), 2, 4, 7, 109, 114.

10   Wil Derske, *A Blessed Life: Benedictine Guidelines for Those Who Long for Good Days* (Collegeville, MN: Liturgical Press, 2009), 58.

11   Mark E. Loltko-Rivera, "Rediscovering the Later Version of Maslow's Hierarchy of Needs: Self-Transcendence and Opportunities for Theory, Research, and Unification," *Review of General Psychology*, Vol. 10, no. 4 (2006): 302–15.

12   John Paul II, *Laborem Exercens* (On Human Work), September 14, 1981. #6, "Work in the Subjective Sense: Man as the Subject of Work."

13   Quote taken from C. Otto Scharmer, *Theory U: Leading from the Future as It Emerges* (Cambridge, MA: Society for Organizational Learning, Inc., 2007), 20.

14   Henri Nouwen, *Reaching Out: The Three Movements of the Spiritual Life* (New York: Image Books [Doubleday], 1975), 71.

15   Joan Chittister, O.S.B., *Wisdom Distilled from the Daily: Living the Rule of St. Benedict Today* (New York: HarperOne, 1991), 83.

16   Ibid.

17   Herbert Applebaum, *The Concept of Work: Ancient, Medieval, and Modern* (Albany, NY: State University of New York Press, 1992), 202.

18   Norvene Vest, *Friend of the Soul: A Benedictine Spirituality of Work* (Boston: Cowley Publications, 1997).

19   Derske, *A Blessed Life*, 54–55.

CHAPTER 1

1   Anselm Grün, *Benedict of Nursia: His Message for Today*, Linda M. Maloney, trans. (Collegeville, MN: Liturgical Press, 2006), 50.

2   Jean Vanier, *Seeing Beyond Depression* (Mahwah, NJ: Paulist Press, 2001), 59.

3   Irshad Manji, *The Trouble with Islam Today: A Muslim's Call for Reform in Her Faith* (New York: St. Martin's Griffin, 2003), 93.

4   Derske, *A Blessed Life*, 58.

5   Eliot, "The Hollow Men."

6   Pierre Teilhard de Chardin, *The Phenomenon of Man*, 2nd ed. (New York: Harper & Row / Harper Torch Book), 1965.

7   Christopher Jamison, O.S.B., *Finding Sanctuary: Monastic Steps for Everyday Life* (London: Phoenix, 2008), 48.

8   These 4 Ps, as we called them, are found in Cox and Rock, *The 7 Pillars of Visionary Leadership*, 15–16.

9   Joan Chittister, *Following the Path: The Search for a Life of Passion, Purpose and Joy* (New York: Image, 2012), 26.

10 Ibid., 47.

11 As "Himself" in "The Muppet Show," episode # 2.19, December 6, 1977.

12 For a very good read on the topic of practice, see Daniel Coyle, *The Talent Code: Greatness Isn't Born. It's Grown. Here's How* (New York: Bantam Books, 2009).

13 Quoted in Tom Keene, "Read and Think Like Mr. Buffet," *Bloomberg Business Week*, August 27, 2013. http://www.businessweek.com/articles/2013-08-27/read-and-think-like-mr-dot-buffett.

14 http://www.goodreads.com/quotes/50584-your-beliefs-become-your-thoughts-your-thoughts-become-your-words. For a YouTube presentation, see https://www.youtube.com/watch?v=cFayOIUHJ-U.

CHAPTER 2

1   Jean Vanier, *Community and Growth*, 2nd rev. ed. (Mahwah, NJ: Paulist Press, 1989), 34.

2   "Patience." Dictionary.com. http://dictionary.reference.com/browse/patience.

3   Second Vatican Council, "Gaudium et Spes," no. 4.

4   In RB 34.6, Benedict is basically telling his monks to be grateful for what they do have, a notion that "flies in the face of that consumerist ideology" that to-day encourages a person to measure their self-worth by their possessions. See Terrence Kardong, *Benedict's Rule: A Translation and Commentary* (Collegeville, MN: The Liturgical Press, 1996), 288.

5   Alisdair McIntyre, *After Virtue: A Study in Moral Theory* (London: Duckworth, 1981), 275.

6   Applebaum, *The Concept of Work*, 202.

CHAPTER 3

1   Marcus Buckingham and Curt W. Coffman, *First, Break All the Rules: What the World's Greatest Managers Do Differently* (New York: Simon & Schuster, 1999), 132.

2   I have taken Benedict's 12 Steps from his Chapter 7 on "Humility" and provided a contemporary understanding.

3   CEO disease is "the information vacuum around a leader created when people withhold important (and usually unpleasant) information." From Daniel Goleman, Richard Boyatzis and Annie McKee, *Primal Leadership: Realizing*

the Power of Emotional Intelligence (Boston: Harvard Business School Press, 2002), 93.

4   "A New Covenant was a political slogan used by U.S. President Bill Clinton to describe his political philosophy and agenda. [Footnote 1] The term was used sporadically during the 1992 campaign and Clinton's terms in office to describe a 'new social compact' between the United States Government and its citizens." "New Covenant," Wikipedia. http://en.wikipedia.org/wiki/New_Covenant_%28politics%29. [Footnote 1]: Clinton, Bill (October 23, 1991). The New Covenant: Responsibility and Rebuilding the American Community (Speech). Georgetown University. See also William J. Clinton, XLII President of the United States: 1993–2001, "Address Accepting the Presidential Nomination at the Democratic National Convention in New York," July 16, 1992.

5   One book that highlights this prevalent notion of acquisitiveness (with many case examples) is Oliver James, *Affluenza: How to Be Successful and Stay Sane* (London: Vermillion, 2007).

6   Ken Wilber, "Taking Responsibility for Your Shadow," in Jeremiah Abrams and Connie Sweig, eds., *Meeting the Shadow: The Hidden Power of the Dark Side of Human Nature* (Los Angeles: Jeremy P. Tarcher, 1991), 274.

7   Ken Wilber, *Integral Spirituality: A Starting New Role for Religion in the Modern and Postmodern World* (Boston, MA: Integral Books, 2006), 121.

8   Margaret Wheatley, *Leadership and the New Science: Learning About Organization from an Orderly Universe* (San Francisco: Berrett-Koehler Publishers, 1992), 144–45.

9   Stephanie T. Solansky, "To Fear Foolishness for the Sake of Wisdom: A Message to Leaders," *Journal of Business Ethics*, Vol. 122, no. 1 (2014): 39–51.

CHAPTER 4

1   Wheatley, *Leadership and the New Science*, 144–45.

2   Moses L. Pava, *The Search for Meaning in Organizations: Seven Practical Questions for Ethical Managers* (Westport, CT: Quorum Books, 1999), 5–6.

3   Solansky, "To Fear Foolishness for the Sake of Wisdom," 39–51.

4   M. Alvesson and A. Spicer, "A Stupidity-Based Theory of Organizations," *Journal of Management Studies*, Vol. 49, no. 7 (2012): 1194–1220. The authors describe being functionally stupid to describe organizations – in our terms, leaders lacking wisdom – who engage in actions without much thought or reasoning or justifying their decisions.

5   I have used a translation by Eugene H. Peterson, *The Message*. Amazon.ca describes Peterson's work as "… a fresh, compelling, insightful, challenging, faith-filled paraphrase of the Bible into contemporary idiomatic American English [that] is first and foremost a reader's Bible."

6   Michael Rock, *Ethics to Live By, to Work By* (Toronto: McGraw-Hill, 2011), 3–6. Out of print. An e-book (.pdf) only now for college/university Business Ethics courses.

7   Adapted from John S. Hammond, Ralph L. Keeney and Howard Raiffa, "The Hidden Traps in Decision Making," *Harvard Business Review*, January 2006, 9 pages. http://www.thinkdsi.com/pdfs/Hidden_Traps_in_Decision_Making.pdf.

8   Solansky, "To Fear Foolishness for the Sake of Wisdom," 45.

CHAPTER 5

1   Bernard McGinn and John Meyendorff in collaboration with Jean Leclercq, "Preface" and "Introduction," xi-xxv, *Christian Spirituality – I: Origins to the Twelfth Century,* Vol. 16 of *World Spirituality: An Encyclopedic History of the Religious Quest* (New York: Crossroad, 1985), 412.

2   Edward Schillebeeckx, O.P., *World and Church*, N.D. Smith, trans. (London: Sheed and Ward, 1971), 1.

3   Quoted in the *The Sun Magazine*, Issue 417, September 2010. http://thesun-magazine.org/issues/417/sunbeams.

4   Aniela Jaffé, recorder and editor, *Memories, Dreams, Reflections by C.G. Jung* (New York: Vintage Books, 1965), 177.

5   Susan Rowland, *Jung as a Writer* (New York: Routledge, 2005), 23.

6   Robyn Reilly, "Five Ways to Improve Employee Engagement Now," *Gallup Business Journal*, January 7, 2014. http://www.gallup.com/businessjournal/166667/five-ways-improve-employee-engagement.aspx.

7   Irene Claremont de Castillejo, *Knowing Woman: A Feminine Psychology* (Boston, MA: Shambhala, 1997), 15. She distinguishes between "focused consciousness" (when things seem sharp and clear) and "diffuse awareness" (when one experiences a sense of unity in awareness). She attributes the contemporary drive of focused consciousness to an attitude embedded in our masculine culture but coming at a cost of the hardening of heart. The Jewish prophet Ezekiel describes this hardening in the image of a "heart of stone" (Ezek. 36:22-28).

CHAPTER 6

1   Reilly, "Five Ways to Improve Employee Engagement Now." Reilly writes, "Engaged workers stand apart from their not-engaged and actively disengaged counterparts because of the discretionary effort they consistently bring to their roles." http://www.gallup.com/businessjournal/166667/five-ways-improve-employee-engagement.aspx.

2   Claudia Heimer, "Emotional Rehydration" [originally in *The Ashbridge Journal*, 6 pages (1999)], in L. Holbeche and N. Springett, *In Search of Meaning in the Workplace* (Horsham, West Sussex: Roffey Park, 2003).

3   St. Benedict would be greatly pleased to read the following results from recent research (2014) completed in India on innovation and organizations. The research validates the many points I have been making in regard to transforming a 'workplace' into a '*worth*place': According to the authors, "The five common practices of implementing innovation culture in order of importance were found to be (1) Core values and beliefs were commonly practiced by all from top to bottom in these organizations. (2) The core values of these organizations define and give shape and clarity of direction to the people in these organizations. (3) These organizations built a culture of openness and transparency. The rewards in these organizations were directly linked to performance of the employees. (4) The human relationships in these organizations are based on the values of care and trust for people in the organization. (5) In these organizations there is consistency between what the top management 'professes' and 'what they actually do.' Senior managers walk their talk." In S. Sai Manohar and Shiv R. Pandit, "Core Values and Beliefs: A Study of Leading Innovative Organizations," *Journal of Business Ethics*, Vol. 125, no. 4 (2014): 678, 679.

4   Danah Zohar and Ian Marshall, *SQ: Connecting with our Spiritual Intelligence* (New York: Bloomsbury, 2000), 16.

5   I extrapolated and intuited the notion of the 'yearning organization' after I read Brian Stanfield, "Mapping the Journey of the Organization," *EDGES*, Vol. 9, no. 2 (August 1997), 7 pages.

6   Michael Rock, "What Is EQ Anyhow? Part 1: Starting the Conversation," *Celebrate!* EQ GOES TO CHURCH series, Vol. 49, no. 1 (Jan/Feb 2010): 40–41.

7   Peter J. Frost, *Toxic Emotions at Work and What You Can Do About Them* (Cambridge, MA: Harvard Business Press, 2007), 213.

8   Cox and Rock, *The 7 Pillars of Visionary Leadership*, 49.

CHAPTER 7

1   For a recently published discussion on values and ethics and how these notions relate to meaningful work as discussed in this book, see Ferdinand Tablan, "Catholic Social Teachings: Toward a Meaningful Work," *Journal of Business Ethics*, Vol. 128, no. 2 (May 2015), 291–303.

2   Quoted from *As a Man Thinketh*, 20. https://wahiduddin.net/thinketh/as_a_man_thinketh.pdf.

3   https://books.google.com/books?id=JrPdhuiSxiMC&pg=PA28&lpg=PA28&dq=We+must+touch+his+weakness+with+a+delicate+hand.+There+are+some+faults&source=bl&ots=97H47HsUMR&sig=wNShBrJ5qYBDQmssEwsIE6wUGao&hl=en&sa=X&ei=66kqVaD7CYfigwT5iIGYBw&ved=0CB8Q6AEwAA#v=onepage&q=We%20must%20touch%20his%20weakness%20with%20a%20delicate%20hand.%20There%20are%20some%20faults&f=false

4   Google News Archive, "Opportunity," *The Free Lance-Star* (Fredericksburg, VA), December 17, 1971, column 7, p. 4.

5   *Nicomachean Ethics,* Book II, 4; Book I, 7.

6   Michele Galen with Karen West, "Companies Hit the Road Less Traveled," *Business Week*, June 5, 1995. http://www.businessweek.com/archives/1995/b342781.arc.htm.

7   Quoted in D.P. Ashmos and D. Duchon, "Spirituality at Work: A Conceptualization and Measure," *Journal of Management Inquiry*, Vol. 9, no. 2 (June 2000): 134.

8   Barry Z. Posner, "Foreword," in Robert A. Giacalone and Carole L. Jurkiewicz, eds., *Handbook of Workplace Spirituality and Organizational Performance* (Armonk, NY: M.E. Sharpe, 2003), xii.

9   Thomas Moore, *Care of the Soul: A Guide for Cultivating Depth and Sacredness in Everyday Life* (New York: HarperCollins, 1992), 181.

10 Giacalone and Jurkiewicz, *Handbook of Workplace Spirituality and Organizational Performance*, 13. Italics in the original. In the second edition of their Handbook, the authors have changed their definition to read: "aspects of the workplace, either in the individual, the group, or the organization, that promote individual feelings of satisfaction through transcendence." Their reasons for this are not set out, and since this is very recent, there has been no opportunity for critical analysis. In Giacalone and Jurkiewicz, eds., *Handbook of Workplace Spirituality and Organizational Performance*, 2nd ed. (Armonk, NY: M.E. Sharpe, 2010), 13.

CHAPTER 8

1   S. Bates, "Getting Engaged: Half of your employees may be just going through the motions," *HR Magazine*, Vol. 49, no. 2 (February 2004): 44–51.

2   Mark Attridge, Joel B. Bennet, Mark C. Frame and James Campbell Quick, "Corporate Health Profile: Measuring Engagement and Presenteeism," in Michael A. Richard, William G. Emener and William S. Hutchinson, Jr., eds., *Employee Assistance Programs: Wellness Enhancement Programming*, 4th ed. (Springfield, IL: Charles C. Thomas Publisher, 2009), 229.

3   Chittister, *Wisdom Distilled from the Daily*, 11.

4   Iris Vilnai-Yavetz and Anat Rafaeli, "Organizational Interactions: A Basic Skeleton with Spiritual Tissue," in Giacalone and Carole L. Jurkiewicz, *Handbook of Workplace Spirituality and Organizational Performance*, 79.

5   Ibid.

6   Ibid.

7   Is it possible that this hint of the 'spiritual' may be precisely the unconscious motivation for an employee to begin to become engaged?

8   Timothy Fry, O.S.B., ed., *RB 1980. The Rule of St. Benedict in English. In Latin and English with Notes* (Collegeville, MN: The Liturgical Press, 1981), 251. "On Sunday all are to be engagd in reading …" (RB 48.22). Interestingly, Benedict writes in Latin, "Dominico item die lectioni vacent omnes…" The word "*vacent*" literally means "to be free for" (from whence we get the word "vacation" in English). In other words, for Benedict, "to be engaged" is to make oneself *deliberately* available for the task at hand (italics added).

9   John O'Donohue, *Anam Cara: A Book of Celtic Wisdom* (New York: HarperCollins, 1997), 30.

CHAPTER 9

1   Wheatley, *Leadership and the New Science*, 144–45.

2   Matthew Kells and Sean McGinn, *The Everyday: Benedictine Life at Mount Saviour Monastery*, Chapter 5, "Work." DVD, 50 min., 2005.

3   See Franco Gandolfi, "HR Strategies that Can Take the Sting out of Downsizing-Related Layoffs," *IVEY Business Journal* (Online), July/Aug 2008. http://iveybusinessjournal.com/topics/strategy/hr-strategies-that-can-take-the-sting-out-of-downsizing-related-layoffs.

4   Moses L. Pava, *The Search for Meaning in Organizations: Seven Practical Questions for Ethical Managers* (Westport, CT): Quorum Books, 1999), 5–6.

5   Dumm, *Cherish Christ Above All*, 114, 115.

6   Arlie Russell Hochschild, *The Managed Heart: Commercialization of Human Feeling*, 2nd ed. (Berkley, CA: University of California Press, [1983] 2003), 134–35.

7   William A. Kahn, "Psychological Conditions of Personal Engagement and Disengagement at Work," *Academy of Management Journal*, Vol. 33, no. 4 (Dec 1990): 692–724, esp. 703–704, 708, 714.

8   Ibid., 694.

9   E-mail from Dr. Reuven Bar-On, October 1, 2010.

10 Chittister, *Wisdom Distilled from the Daily*, p. 11. Italics added.

11 In Jonathan Montaldo, ed., *Thomas Merton: Choosing to Love the World* (Boulder, CO: Sounds True, 2008), 37.

CHAPTER 10

1   Reilly, "Five Ways to Improve Employee Engagement Now."

2   "Easing the Strain a National Focus," *National Post*, Oct. 6, 2011, p. JV3.

3   Kathryn May, "Ottawa 'Depression Capital of Canada,'" *Ottawa Citizen*, Sept. 22, 2010.

4   Kees Waaijman, *Spirituality: Forms, Foundations, Methods*, John Vriend, trans. *Studies in Spirituality. Supplement 8* (Leuven: Peeters, Bondgenotenlaan 153, B-3000, 2002), 1.

5   Brian Draper, *Spiritual Intelligence: A New Way of Being* (Oxford: A Lion Book, 2009), 18.

6   http://www.nationalmuseum.af.mil/factsheets/factsheet.asp?id=1349.

7   Edwin Shneidman, *Voices of Death: Letters, Diaries and Other Personal Documents for People Facing Death that Provide Comforting Guidance for Each of Us* (New York: Harper and Row, 1980), 112.

8   Vest, *Friend of the Soul*, 1.

9   Chittister, *Wisdom Distilled from the* Daily, 83.

10 Mayeul de Dreuile, O.S.B., *The Rule of Saint Benedict: A Commentary in Light of World Ascetic Traditions* (New York/Mahwah, NJ: The Newman Press, 2000), 232.

11 Daryl Koehn, "The Soul's Hunger: Spirituality in Corporations and in the Teaching of Business Ethics," *Research in Ethical Issues in Organizations*, Vol. 12 (2003): 7.

INDEX

for life, 25; as quiet background force, 90

stabilitas (stability), 15, 21, 24, 26, 56, 74, 83, 97; and maturity, 23

stakeholders, 82

standards, prevailing, 45

status quo, 48

sticks and stones, 30

stillness, 52, 53

straight lines, 57

strategies, thought-out, 31

street sweeper (Martin Luther King quote), 65

strengths, others', 61

stubbornness, innate, 37

stupid, functionally, 46

subjective dimension, 14, 91, 92, 95

subsidiarity, 17

sunk cost, 48

surprises in our lives, God's, 32

survival and Darwin, 12

sweetness of love, unspeakable (P49), 17

swelled head, 37

synergy, 82

T

T.S. Eliot, 11

tapestry of true listening, 56, 88

tardiness, 98

teamwork, 62

technical competencies, 31, 92

Teresa of Avila, 39

texting, 31

thirst for identity, 67

thoughts, 52, 83

tilt (*Confessions*, I, 1), 60

time and meaning, 22

tips, twelve concrete, 37

tissue vs. skeleton scripts, 76

tongue, 42; and evil, 30

Tools of Good Works, 97

toxicity, 32; relationships, 44; senior manager (Ryan), 11; work environment, 75

training manual, the *Rule*, 70

tranquility, 52

transcendence, 13, 53, 59, 60, 61, 79, 91, 69; and connectedness, 20; *transcendere*, 91

transparency, 39

transpersonal, 60

traps, decision, 50

trials and errors, many, 37

trust, authority by, 46

truth and meaning, kernel, 38

turning point, 8

Twitter, 28

two hearts beating as one, 37

U

ultimacy, 60

unconscious contents, projection of, 29, 37; destabilizing presence of, 55

understanding *and* acceptance, 51, 53

unhappiness, 21

uniqueness, thirst for, 67

universe and work, 20

unjust treatment, dealing with, 54

unmasking self to self, 25

unspeakable sweetness of love (P49), 17

urban hesychast, 52

V

Valéry, Paul, 26

value path, 40; skewed, 63

values, 8; external and quantitative, 31; internal and qualitative, 31

Vanier, Jean, 23, 28

variety in work, 86

vessel, break the, 30; sacred (RB 31.10), 91

Vest, Norvene, 19

virtue and vice, 67